CASES IN ACCOUNTING ETHICS & PROFESSIONALISM

THIRD EDITION

●●●●●●●●●●●●●

STEVEN M. MINTZ

Dean of the School of Business
California State University, San Bernardino

The McGraw-Hill Companies, Inc.

New York St. Louis San Francisco Auckland Bogotá
Caracas Lisbon London Madrid Mexico City Milan Montreal
New Delhi San Juan Singapore Sydney Tokyo Toronto

McGraw-Hill

A Division of The **McGraw·Hill** *Companies*

1 2 3 4 5 6 7 8 9 0 DOC DOC 9 0 3 2 1 0 9 8 7 6

ISBN 0-07-042834-4

Library of Congress Cataloging-in-Publication Data

Mintz, Steven M.
    Cases in accounting ethics and professionalism/Steven M. Mintz.
  —3rd ed.
      p.   cm.
    ISBN 0-07-042834-4
    1. Accountants—Professional ethics—United States—Case studies.
I. Title.
HF5616.U5M534   1997
174´.9657—dc20   96-22830
                                                  CIP

This book was set in Times Roman by ComCom.
The editors were Alan Sachs and Terri Wicks.
The production supervisor was Louis Swaim.
The cover was designed by Nadja Lazansky.
This book was printed and bound by RR Donnelley.

About the Author

■

STEVEN M. MINTZ, D.B.A., CPA, is the dean of the School of Business and Public Administration at California State University, San Bernardino. Previously, Dr. Mintz was a professor of accounting and the Department Chair at Southwest Texas State University (1990–1996) and a professor of accounting and the Department Chair at San Francisco State University (1981–1990). Dr. Mintz received his Doctor of Business Administration degree in 1978 from George Washington University. He is also a Certified Public Accountant in New York State.

Dr. Mintz has served on the Professional Ethics Committees of the California and Texas Societies of CPAs. He developed and teaches a continuing education course in ethics for CPAs in Texas. The course was instrumental in leading to a 1995 mandate of the Texas State Board of Public Accountancy declaring that CPAs in Texas must have four hours of continuing education in ethics every three years as a condition of relicensing.

Dr. Mintz has presented ethics training programs to a variety of business organizations and government agencies. He has researched and spoken extensively on the need to teach accounting ethics and professionalism. Dr. Mintz has had more than 20 research papers published on a variety of issues related to professional ethics and the philosophy of ethics.

The California Society of CPAs honored Dr. Mintz for his contributions to the development of the accounting profession and his influence on its future members by selecting him as the recipient of the 1988 Faculty Excellence Award.

This book is dedicated
to my parents, who taught
me right from wrong
at an early age, and to my
wife, Paula, and daughter,
Rebecca, who
demonstrate a commitment
to ethical behavior in so
many things that they do.

I hope the book serves to inspire
students to strive for excellence
in whatever they do and to always
be sensitive to the ethical issues.

Contents

■

Bubba Tech, Inc. (BTI)   **71**

Role and responsibilities of top management and the audit committee in initiating a competitive bidding process for the selection
of external auditors.

Linex Corporation   **76**

Ethical and professional issues related to a change of auditors
resulting from a difference of opinion with a client about proper
disclosure of a litigation uncertainty in the financial statements.

Edvid, Inc.   **78**

Application of the ethical decision-making process when there is
a difference of opinion with client management over proper revenue recognition and related effects on the quarterly reports.

Engineering Associates   **85**

Conflicts with an MAS client caused by poor operating and oversight techniques in the installation of an information system.

Compu-View   **90**

Evaluating the ethics of issuing a review report, a compilation
report, or no report with assembled financial statements, in light
of client concerns about possible investor reactions to disclosures about improper accounting for research and development
costs.

Financial, Inc.   **94**

Operating-loss carrybacks and carryforwards of a consolidated
entity and related ethical considerations in taking a tax position
under the "realistic possibility standard."

Cubbies Cable   **98**

Ethical analysis of the positions taken by the external auditors
and client management when there is a difference of opinion
over how to recognize revenue on a sale-leaseback transaction.

Classic Silk Clothiers, Inc.   **106**

Loyalty conflict for the external auditors when the chairperson of
the audit committee requests that the auditors investigate the
travel and entertainment expenditures of the top officers.

Foreword

■

This is an important and much-needed book.

As Dr. Steven Mintz makes clear in his introduction, these are extraordinarily complicated and precarious times for the accounting profession. Perhaps more than ever before there is a need for men and women of scrupulous integrity to design, oversee, report, and audit the records and reports of business, government, and the nonprofit sector. But it isn't getting any easier. Young people entering the profession absolutely need the opportunity this book affords if they are to learn to recognize and deal with the myriad of ethical challenges they are likely to face.

In the last few decades, technological developments have enabled organizations to generate virtually instantaneous current reports on anything that can be counted. At the same time, new demands for profitability and productivity have, along with the emergence of management theories such as management by objective (MBO), and total quality management (TQM), placed a huge emphasis on setting and hitting numerical goals as a means of measuring success and determining compensation. This has created a numbers-driven culture in both the business and public sectors, a culture that provides seemingly endless opportunities and incentives for distortion and outright fraud.

Add to this mix the vast changes in the accounting profession itself—including intense competition, the proliferation of new services provided to clients, the promulgation of new ethical and professional standards, and more extensive and complicated laws regulating record-keeping and reporting—and one can see why there is unprecedented pressure on the integrity of individuals and systems.

The stakes have never been higher nor the risks associated with unethical conduct greater. It is not enough that accountants refuse to participate in false and misleading activities of their clients and employers. To an increasing degree, they are held accountable to prevent, detect, and report all manner of actual and potential improprieties.

A growing body of laws and regulations impose obligations on organizations to monitor and report on internal matters. For example, the Foreign Corrupt Practices Act, which outlaws bribes in foreign countries, places heavy systems-design and auditing responsibilities on companies. The more recent Federal Sentencing Guidelines, which govern illegal acts by agents of corporations and other organizations, add a wide range of new penalties and self-reporting strictures that require rigorous management oversight and proactive defensive measures, such as education and training. Some new laws demand that organizations turn themselves in to government regulators when they discover illegal behavior within the organization. And new legislation, especially in the areas of environmental mandates and the regulation of the financial services industry, requires high-level executives to personally certify that their organization is in full compliance with applicable rules. These certifications subject both the executives and their organizations to stiff penalties for false or inaccurate statements.

In this setting, the accountant is likely to be confronted with the need to perceive and overcome any incentives to subordinate ethical considerations to short-term organizational interests. It is never easy to bite the hand that feeds you, and, in the real world, where everyone has bills and career ambitions, ethical commitment is frequently tested. In this context, there is no immunity from the pressure to go along, to look the other way, or to rationalize questionable behavior. It often takes great character to do the right thing and to demand that others do so.

Moreover, the accountant's work is subject to unprecedented public scrutiny. It is a time of aggressive investigative reporting by sophisticated journalists who know how to find and analyze numbers. Downsizing, right-sizing, and reengineering have caused thousands of white-collar workers to lose their jobs, and many of them are disgruntled and hostile to their former employers. This has generated an army of potential whistle-blowers who are ready to reveal any hanky-panky within an organization.

The penchant of modern corporations, government entities, and charities to base almost all important decisions on data magnifies the need to assure that the data are reliable. To be reliable, the information must be complete and accurate. Outright dishonest reporting, as well as inadvertent errors and omissions, must be discouraged and detected. Surveys by the Josephson Institute of Ethics indicate that the internal reports depended on by management are often inaccurate. For example, in a typical company, at least one in five managers admits to having lied to or deceived a superior within the previous 12 months and about one in three managers says that there is a kill-the-messenger syndrome in their organization that "causes employees to conceal or distort negative information." The tendency to "tailor facts" to tell management what it wants to hear is another factor that challenges the integrity of vital decision-making documents.

Finally, accounting professionals must take into account the well-documented decline in the ethical values of the next generation of employers, coworkers, clients, and regulators. According to a 1996 study by the Joseph and Edna Josephson Institute of Ethics, 4 in 10 high schoolers admit to having stolen something from a store and two-thirds admit to having cheated on an exam—all within the previous 12 months. More than half also said they would lie to get or keep a job.

The formal and informal standards of ethics and professional conduct explored in this book are vital safeguards. Yet, in the last analysis, external standards will have no serious impact unless the professionals asked to uphold them have and demonstrate the strong personal and professional conscience needed to drive an internal commitment to both do the right thing and do it right. Conscientious study of the materials in this book should help.

Michael Josephson

President
Joseph and Edna Josephson Institute of Ethics

Preface

■

Cases in this book depict a variety of situations where accountants and auditors have to decide complex issues based on professional and ethical standards. The cases are divided into four sections, each dealing with a different type of case: (1) human resource issues, (2) external reporting cases, (3) internal reporting cases, and (4) cases in the international environment. Brief descriptions of the substance of each case appear in the Contents. The *Instructor's Manual* contains a matrix that shows how I think the cases might be used to integrate ethics into the accounting curriculum.

Most of the cases in the book are based on actual dilemmas encountered by public accountants, internal auditors, or management accountants. Special recognition is due all the accounting professionals who freely gave of their time and energies in discussing with me some of the most difficult experiences that they encountered on the job. Their candidness and professionalism was a constant source of encouragement for me in this project. All cases are disguised, in order to provide anonymity for the individuals and organizations involved.

PURPOSE OF THE BOOK

The purpose of this book is to provide a group of cases that will serve not only as the basis for a course in ethics and professionalism, but also as the basis for the consideration of ethics and professionalism in a variety of accounting courses. Additionally, one section of the book provides a philosophical framework that relies on the application of moral reasoning in order to resolve ethical dilemmas. The material in this section should be used to analyze the ethical issues that arise in all 25 cases in the book.

Auditing courses at both the graduate and the undergraduate level and senior-level undergraduate and graduate accounting theory and policy seminars are ideal places in the curriculum for the integration of these cases. At the same time, many of the cases can be used in other accounting courses, such as intermediate financial accounting and advanced cost or management accounting courses. Many cases can be used in introductory undergraduate and graduate-level accounting courses in order to expose all business students to ethical and professional issues of concern to accountants. In particular, the new cases that explore human resource decisions emphasize the culture of public accounting firms and the expectations of accounting employers for the ethical behavior of employees. Finally, a new section of the book presents three cases in which international issues are raised. The cases in this section focus on issues such as transfer pricing, making payments to foreign officials in order to obtain business, and relevant provisions of the Foreign Corrupt Practices Act. Each of the two new sections contains background material that describes some of the more important ethical issues that are included in the cases in these sections. This material has been omitted from the Introduction section of the casebook in order to facilitate either coverage of the material in a course or exclusion of the material from a course.

Two other sections contain cases that are categorized as external reporting or internal reporting, respectively, based on the perspective of the accountant facing the ethical dilemma. For example, the Sweat Hog Construction Company case describes the ethical conflict of a controller who disagrees with the president about the proper application of the percentage-of-completion method of recognizing revenue. Although this case is classified as internal, it could be assigned in an intermediate accounting class. Faculty are encouraged to decide on course assignments of the cases only after considering the descriptions in the Contents and the course classification matrix in the *Instructor's Manual.* Students might find it helpful to refer back to the Introduction section of the casebook for guidance on resolving ethical conflicts that arise in the external and internal accounting environments.

CHANGES IN THIS EDITION

The third edition of this book differs from the second edition in five important ways. First, this edition contains 11 additional cases. Some of these cases focus on ethical considerations in selecting appropriate accounting principles. The objective of these cases is to enable faculty to discuss ethical issues while reinforcing basic accounting concepts such as revenue recognition and asset valuation. As previously mentioned, there are two new sections in the book. The cases in the section on human resource decisions, such as how an accounting firm evaluates the performance of its employees, raise ethical issues that should be of concern to all accounting students. The increased globalization of business operations creates a need to expose accounting students to the ethical dimension of operating abroad, which is discussed in the other new section.

The second improvement is the incorporation of virtue ethics into the ethical analysis material in the philosophical framework section of the book. There is a renewed interest in the ancient Greek concept of virtue as an approach to ethical reasoning. Virtue ethics is different from the other reasoning methods discussed in the philosophical framework section. The virtue ethics method focuses both on the *agent* and the decision to be made by the agent, whereas the other methods emphasize certain criteria that guide decision making by the agent.

The third improvement is the expansion of the variety of cases in the external and internal reporting areas. For example, two new cases focus on the misuse of organizational resources by members of top management. Although the issue involved borders on legality, and some faculty may find it more clear-cut than most ethical dilemmas, the implications of such actions by members of top management can create ethical pressures for industry accountants. Students should benefit from a discussion of the conflict that exists for industry accountants who have an obligation to be loyal to their employer but who also are expected to make decisions that are in the public interest.

The fourth improvement is the provision of tools to assist students in analyzing the facts and in making decisions. This adds structure to the case assignments. The ethical decision-making process that is presented in the third section should help students to organize their thoughts in responding to case questions. The Questronics case provides an opportunity for students to familiarize themselves with the analysis of ethical issues using an uncomplicated set of facts. Analyzing this relatively straightforward sample case should enable students to deal more effectively with the more complicated factual situations in the 25 real-life–based cases.

The final improvement is the inclusion of new end-of-text assignments that are designed to provide additional source material for faculty. These assignments can be used (1) as the basis for research projects on materiality that tie together the ethical dimension of materiality judgments covered in some of the cases; (2) for testing purposes, group discussions, or presentations of ethical issues; or (3) to engage students in role-playing exercises. The virtue ethics material is a good example of a method of ethical analysis that can benefit from experiential learning techniques, such as role-playing. Faculty may want to add role-playing exercises to the assigned questions at the end of some of the cases in order to enhance the learning experience.

The *Instructor's Manual* that accompanies the casebook contains additional questions that can be used to extend the boundaries of selected cases. Faculty are encouraged to develop their own additional case assignments in order to meet the needs of their students. Some faculty may want to assign the materiality research project early in the course, before assigning cases—such as Linex, Classic Silk Clothiers, and Supreme Designs—that raise the materiality issue. There are six cases in the *Instructor's Manual* that can be duplicated for students and used as additional assignments or for testing purposes. (These cases were in the second edition but have been moved to the *Instructor's Manual* in the third edition to make room for the new cases. Some of the case material has been changed to enhance potential discussions with students.)

One of the goals of integrating ethics into the curriculum is to expose accounting students to a variety of ethical dilemmas they might face on the job. After accounting students graduate from universities, some go to work in public accounting whereas others enter private industry. Many will switch from one field to the other. Faculty are encouraged to experiment with a variety of cases in a given course in order to develop students' skills in evaluating alternative courses of ethical action and as a way of sensitizing students to ethical issues they may face at one point or another in their accounting careers.

ACKNOWLEDGMENTS

I extend my sincere appreciation to the College Division of McGraw-Hill and its excellent editorial staff including Alan Sachs, Executive Editor, and Kezia Pearlman, Editorial Assistant, for their responsiveness and professionalism in helping me to develop the manuscript. I would also like to express my appreciation to the production staff for its outstanding work in editing the manuscript for the third edition. In particular, I would like to thank Terri Wicks, Editing Supervisor, and Louis Swaim, Production Supervisor, from the San Francisco office, along with copyeditor Zaza Ziemba and proofreader Joan Bosi.

I would like to acknowledge my gratitude to the American Accounting Association for permitting me to use a figure from my manuscript on virtue ethics that appeared in *Issues in Accounting Education* (Fall 1995). Thanks also go to the American Institute of Certified Public Accountants for permitting me to reproduce material in the Introduction from *Statement on Auditing Standards No. 58 and No. 59* and *The Code of Professional Conduct*. I would like to also thank the Institute of Management Accountants and the Institute of Internal Auditors for allowing me to reproduce their codes of ethics. Johnson and Johnson should be recognized for granting permission to reproduce their Credo. I also acknowledge the Financial Accounting Standards Board for its permission to reproduce material in the Edvid, Inc., case from *Statement of Financial Accounting Standards No. 48 and No. 53* and in the Cubbies Cable case from *Statement of Financial Accounting Standards No. 28, 29, and 51.** I appreciate the cooperation of each of these organizations and of Dow Jones & Company, Inc., in allowing me to reproduce certain material and accounting standards in the *Instructor's Manual*.

Recognition is also due Dr. Richard J. Boland, Jr., professor of management information and decision systems at Case Western Reserve University. Dr. Boland graciously consented to my use of one of his cases, Video Concepts, Inc., which was included in a 1982 manuscript titled *Cases in Accounting Policy and Practice.* That case has been expanded and updated and is here referred to as *Edvid, Inc.*

---

*Copyright by Financial Accounting Standards Board (FASB), 401 Merritt 7, P.O. Box 5116, Norwalk, Connecticut, 06856-5116, U.S.A. Reprinted with permission. Copies of the complete document are available from the FASB.

I am indebted to the many students and faculty at Southwest Texas State University who provided valuable comments on the cases that were included in the second edition of the book. I am also very grateful to Dr. Robert C. Fess, a retired professor from San Francisco State University, and Dr. Dianna Ross Coker, an assistant professor at St. Mary's University in San Antonio, Texas, for their very helpful comments on the first draft of the material in the 11 new cases included in this edition. My appreciation also goes to several anonymous reviewers who evaluated the material in the second edition and the new material in the third edition. Their comments were very helpful in sharpening the focus of the cases and in strengthening the questions at the end of the cases.

A final thank you to Robert E. Knox, who recently retired as the director of relations with educators for the California Society of CPAs. Bob's support in developing cases for the first edition of the book was instrumental in getting me on the road to developing the more sophisticated material in the third edition of the book.

As is true in any project of this kind, ultimate responsibility for any deficiencies in this book must be assumed by the author.

Steven M. Mintz

INTRODUCTION

In 1987 the accounting profession in the United States celebrated its one-hundredth anniversary. One of the most significant events during that period was the evolution of *The Code of Professional Conduct of the American Institute of Certified Public Accountants* (AICPA). The Code first appeared in its current format in 1973. The code of ethics that exists today[1] is a codification of standards, opinions, rulings, and interpretations of rules of conduct published by the Institute over many years. It reflects the public accounting profession's responses to the expectations and challenges created by itself, the business community, regulators, and other users of financial statements who rely on AICPA members' independence, integrity, objectivity, and adherence to professional standards.

On January 12, 1988, the membership of the AICPA approved changes in the bylaws. These changes stipulate that new members joining the AICPA after the year 2000 must complete 150 semester hours of education, including attainment of a baccalaureate degree or its equivalent. The increased education requirement has prompted many accounting educators and professionals to call for more ethics education in the university curriculum.

The issue of integrating ethics into the accounting curriculum has received increased attention since 1986. In that year, the American Accounting Association (AAA) Committee on the Future Structure, Content, and Scope of Accounting Education (the Bedford Committee) issued a report that stated, "Professional accounting education must not only emphasize the needed skills and knowledge, it must also instill the ethical standards and the commitment of a professional." The National Commission on Fraudulent Financial Reporting (the Treadway Commission) recommended in its 1987 report that, "The business and accounting cur-

---

[1] American Institute of Certified Public Accountants, *Code of Professional Conduct as Amended January 14, 1992* (New York: AICPA, 1994).

ricula should emphasize ethical values by integrating their development with the acquisition of knowledge and skills to help prevent, detect, and deter fraudulent financial reporting." In its 1988 and 1992 reports on the education required in order to become a CPA, the AICPA recommended the integration of ethics in the general education, business administration, and accounting curricula. These reports emphasize the importance of developing ethical values in the accounting student and integrating the coverage of ethical issues with the coverage of technical knowledge throughout the curriculum. In April 1989 the chief executives of the then Big Eight accounting firms issued a position paper, "Perspectives on Education: Capabilities for Success in the Accounting Profession," that presents the firms' view that successful public accountants must be able to identify ethical issues and apply a value-based reasoning system to ethical questions. In September 1990 the Accounting Education Change Commission (AECC) issued a position statement stating that accounting graduates "should know and understand the ethics of the profession and be able to make value-based judgments. They should be prepared to address issues with integrity, objectivity, competence, and concern for the public interest."

The need for teaching ethics as part of the curriculum is evident from the number of businesses and savings and loan institutions that have engaged in fraudulent accounting and financial reporting practices. Two examples from the business community, MiniScribe and the Regina Company, are indicative of the nature of such practices. In both companies, top corporate officials engaged in fraudulent activities, including shipping obsolete or defective merchandise and recording revenue in advance of shipments or for greater amounts of merchandise than were ordered. In both instances the external auditors failed to uncover the fraud.

The cost to the public to clean up the 717 failed savings and loan institutions has been reported to be about $145 billion. However, William Seidman, the former chairman of the Federal Deposit Insurance Corporation (FDIC), estimates the true cost to be closer to $400 billion when the cost of 30 years' interest on the money borrowed to finance the cleanup is included. One of the more publicized failures is that of Lincoln Savings & Loan. Thousands of California retirees lost their life savings after buying uninsured subordinated debentures issued by Lincoln's parent company, American Continental, and sold through Lincoln branches. Arthur Young & Co. (now Ernst & Young), the auditors of American Continental, issued unqualified opinions on the entity's financial statements for fiscal years 1986 and 1987. The audit opinions were part of the annual reports of American Continental that were furnished prospective buyers of the worthless debentures.

The cost to the accounting profession for its role in the savings and loan scandals is evidenced by the fact that all of the Big Six firms have been sued for their involvement in the failures. Three accounting firms settled lawsuits in the Lincoln case by agreeing to pay a total of about $160 million. In 1992, Ernst & Young settled federal charges that the firm inadequately audited four large thrifts that failed— at a cost to the government of $6.6 billion—by agreeing to pay $400 million. The $400 million is the largest settlement the government has won against professionals who failed to follow rules designed to alert regulators and stockholders to problems with the safety and soundness at federally insured depository institutions.

Perhaps no one example of fraudulent financial practices better illustrates the importance of establishing an ethical culture within an organization than the case of Phar-Mor. In 1992 it was revealed that Michael Monus, the president of Phar-Mor, falsified the company's books from June 1989 to July 1992 by overstating inventory and accounts receivable by $499 million. In December 1995, Monus was sentenced to nearly 20 years in prison for fraud and fined $1 million. Patrick Finn, the chief financial officer (CFO), also participated in the scheme. He received a 33-month jail sentence for his role in the fraud. Other members of top management apparently knew of the fraud but kept quiet in an effort to receive more lucrative salaries and bonuses. Phar-Mor sued its outside auditors, Coopers & Lybrand, for failing to uncover the fraud. Coopers filed a countersuit against the company charging it was unable to accurately audit the company's financial statements because they were altered by top executives. Coopers & Lybrand claimed that responsibility rested with the chief executive officer (CEO) and the chairman of the board, who are obligated to manage the company and be familiar with its activities. Ultimately, Phar-Mor removed itself from the federal suit against Coopers and Coopers dropped its countersuit against Phar-Mor, when the two reached a settlement. The terms of the settlement were not disclosed. In February 1996, a federal jury found Coopers liable to a group of investors for failing to uncover the fraud. The plaintiffs are expected to be awarded damages ranging from $50 to $150 billion. Coopers plans to appeal the decision, claiming it was singled out because of its "deep pockets."

An important development in the accounting profession's efforts to limit accountants' liability when lawyers target them because of their ability to pay occurred in December 1995. At that time Congress overrode President Clinton's veto of a bill that is intended to reduce the number of frivolous class-action securities lawsuits. The new law, The Private Securities Litigation Reform Act of 1995, implements a system of proportionate liability whereby less culpable defendants will pay a proportionate (that is, smaller) share of the damages, whereas parties that knowingly engage in fraud will be subject to the full force of joint and several liability.

The problem of fraudulent financial transactions took on an international dimension in the case of The Bank of Credit and Commerce International (BCCI). In July 1991 the Luxembourg unit of the bank collapsed as the result of a multibillion-dollar fraud. In connection with the fraud, Price Waterhouse was named in lawsuits in both Britain and the United States. The firm contends it was a victim of the fraud perpetrated by the highest levels of BCCI's management with the help of third parties that provided false confirmations to the auditors on fictitious and nonrecourse loans. BCCI was charged with falsifying book entries and making payments to silence the would-be whistle-blowers. Price Waterhouse reported that the false and misleading transactions were thought to be limited in extent and that the responsible parties were to be removed. To support this, they cited discussions with the Bank of England and the footnoting of pledges from the Abu Dhabi government (the majority shareholder) to restructure the bank and supply new capital to indemnify against any losses.

Instances of improper financial transactions are not limited to financial statement manipulations. In a 1994 study the Association of Certified Fraud Examiners found that U.S. businesses and organizations lost more than $400 billion through embezzlement that year because their money was diverted for someone's personal use. When employees or executives use company funds under their control for personal purposes, they violate the trust that must exist between an entity and its members.

ETHICS AND PROFESSIONALISM

The term *ethics* refers to a system or code of conduct based on moral duties and obligations that indicates how we should behave; it deals with the ability to distinguish right from wrong and the commitment to do what is right. *Professionalism* refers to the conduct, aims, or qualities that characterize or mark a profession or a professional person. The cornerstone qualities of accounting professionals are competence, objectivity, and integrity. Accounting professionals are guided in their behavior by the provisions of a code of ethics that has been established by professional associations.

The AICPA's *Code of Professional Conduct* applies to all members of the Institute—including those in public practice, industry, government, and education—in the performance of their professional responsibilities. The code consists of two sections: (1) the principles and (2) the rules. The principles are goal-oriented and provide the framework for the profession's technical standards and ethics rules. The principles prescribe the ethical responsibilities members should strive to achieve and express the profession's recognition of its responsibilities to the public, to clients, and to colleagues. The principles call for an unswerving commitment to honorable behavior, even at the sacrifice of personal advantage. The rules represent the enforceable provisions of the Code. However, as is the case with any set of rules, the AICPA's rules can never be expected to anticipate every situation that may be encountered by a professional. Therefore, when the rules are unclear, it is the principles, along with ethical reasoning, that should guide the professional's actions to conform with the "spirit" or intent of the rules.

There are six principles of professional conduct in the code. They deal with (1) the members' responsibilities as professionals, (2) their obligation to act in a way that serves the public interest, (3) the need for the highest sense of integrity in the performance of professional services, (4) the need for objectivity and for independence in the performance of auditing and other attestation services, (5) the need to exercise due care in performing services, and (6) the requirement that members in public practice observe the principles of the code in determining the scope and nature of services to be provided. A summary of the principles appears in Exhibit 1 on pages 5–9.

EXHIBIT 1

AICPA

American Institute of Certified Public Accountants

Code of Professional Conduct

as amended January 14, 1992

Section I—Principles

Preamble

Membership in the American Institute of Certified Public Accountants is voluntary. By accepting membership, a certified public accountant assumes an obligation of self-discipline above and beyond the requirements of laws and regulations.

These Principles of the Code of Professional Conduct of the American Institute of Certified Public Accountants express the profession's recognition of its responsibilities to the public, to clients, and to colleagues. They guide members in the performance of their professional responsibilities and express the basic tenets of ethical and professional conduct. The Principles call for an unswerving commitment to honorable behavior, even at the sacrifice of personal advantage.

Article I
Responsibilities

In carrying out their responsibilities as professionals, members should exercise sensitive professional and moral judgments in all their activities.

(continued)

As professionals, certified public accountants perform an essential role in society. Consistent with that role, members of the American Institute of Certified Public Accountants have responsibilities to all those who use their professional services. Members also have a continuing responsibility to cooperate with each other to improve the art of accounting, maintain the public's confidence, and carry out the profession's special responsibilities for self-governance. The collective efforts of all members are required to maintain and enhance the traditions of the profession.

Article II
The Public Interest

Members should accept the obligation to act in a way that will serve the public interest, honor the public trust, and demonstrate commitment to professionalism.

A distinguishing mark of a profession is acceptance of its responsibility to the public. The accounting profession's public consists of clients, credit grantors, governments, employers, investors, the business and financial community, and others who rely on the objectivity and integrity of certified public accountants to maintain the orderly functioning of commerce. This reliance imposes a public interest responsibility on certified public accountants. The public interest is defined as the collective well-being of the community of people and institutions the profession serves.

In discharging their professional responsibilities, members may encounter conflicting pressures from among each of those groups. In resolving those conflicts, members should act with integrity, guided by the precept that when members fulfill their responsibility to the public, clients' and employers' interests are best served.

Those who rely on certified public accountants expect them to discharge their responsibilities with integrity, objectivity, due professional care, and a genuine interest in serving the public. They are expected to provide quality services, enter into fee arrangements, and offer a range of services—all in a manner that demonstrates a level of professionalism consistent with these Principles of the Code of Professional Conduct.

All who accept membership in the American Institute of Certified Public Accountants commit themselves to honor the public trust. In return for the faith that the public reposes in them, members should seek continually to demonstrate their dedication to professional excellence.

Article III
Integrity

To maintain and broaden public confidence, members should perform all professional responsibilities with the highest sense of integrity.

Integrity is an element of character fundamental to professional recognition. It is the quality from which the public trust derives and the benchmark against which a member must ultimately test all decisions.

(continued)

Integrity requires a member to be, among other things, honest and candid within the constraints of client confidentiality. Service and the public trust should not be subordinated to personal gain and advantage. Integrity can accommodate the inadvertent error and the honest difference of opinion; it cannot accommodate deceit or subordination of principle.

Integrity is measured in terms of what is right and just. In the absence of specific rules, standards, or guidance, or in the face of conflicting opinions, a member should test decisions and deeds by asking: "Am I doing what a person of integrity would do? Have I retained my integrity?" Integrity requires a member to observe both the form and the spirit of technical and ethical standards; circumvention of those standards constitutes subordination of judgment.

Integrity also requires a member to observe the principles of objectivity and independence and of due care.

Article IV
Objectivity and Independence

A member should maintain objectivity and be free of conflicts of interest in discharging professional responsibilities. A member in public practice should be independent in fact and appearance when providing auditing and other attestation services.

Objectivity is a state of mind, a quality that lends value to a member's services. It is a distinguishing feature of the profession. The principle of objectivity imposes the obligation to be impartial, intellectually honest, and free of conflicts of interest. Independence precludes relationships that may appear to impair a member's objectivity in rendering attestation services.

Members often serve multiple interests in many different capacities and must demonstrate their objectivity in varying circumstances. Members in public practice render attest, tax, and management advisory services. Other members prepare financial statements in the employment of others, perform internal auditing services, and serve in financial and management capacities in industry, education, and government. They also educate and train those who aspire to admission into the profession. Regardless of service or capacity, members should protect the integrity of their work, maintain objectivity, and avoid any subordination of their judgment.

For a member in public practice, the maintenance of objectivity and independence requires a continuing assessment of client relationships and public responsibility. Such a member who provides auditing and other attestation services should be independent in fact and appearance. In providing all other services, a member should maintain objectivity and avoid conflicts of interest.

Although members not in public practice cannot maintain the appearance of independence, they nevertheless have the responsibility to maintain objectivity in rendering professional services. Members employed by others to prepare financial statements or to perform auditing, tax, or consulting services are charged with the same responsibility for objectivity as members in public practice and must be

(continued)

scrupulous in their application of generally accepted accounting principles and candid in all their dealings with members in public practice.

Article V
Due Care

A member should observe the profession's technical and ethical standards, strive continually to improve competence and the quality of services, and discharge professional responsibility to the best of the member's ability.

The quest for excellence is the essence of due care. Due care requires a member to discharge professional responsibilities with competence and diligence. It imposes the obligation to perform professional services to the best of a member's ability with concern for the best interest of those for whom the services are performed and consistent with the profession's responsibility to the public.

Competence is derived from a synthesis of education and experience. It begins with a mastery of the common body of knowledge required for designation as a certified public accountant. The maintenance of competence requires a commitment to learning and professional improvement that must continue throughout a member's professional life. It is a member's individual responsibility. In all engagements and in all responsibilities, each member should undertake to achieve a level of competence that will assure that the quality of the member's services meets the high level of professionalism required by these Principles.

Competence represents the attainment and maintenance of a level of understanding and knowledge that enables a member to render services with facility and acumen. It also establishes the limitations of a member's capabilities by dictating that consultation or referral may be required when a professional engagement exceeds the personal competence of a member or a member's firm. Each member is responsible for assessing his or her own competence—of evaluating whether education, experience, and judgment are adequate for the responsibility to be assumed.

Members should be diligent in discharging responsibilities to clients, employers, and the public. Diligence imposes the responsibility to render services promptly and carefully, to be thorough, and to observe applicable technical and ethical standards.

Due care requires a member to plan and supervise adequately any professional activity for which he or she is responsible.

Article VI
Scope and Nature of Services

A member in public practice should observe the Principles of the Code of Professional Conduct in determining the scope and nature of services to be provided.

(continued)

The public interest aspect of certified public accountants' services requires that such services be consistent with acceptable professional behavior for certified public accountants. Integrity requires that service and the public trust not be subordinated to personal gain and advantage. Objectivity and independence require that members be free from conflicts of interest in discharging professional responsibilities. Due care requires that services be provided with competence and diligence.

Each of these Principles should be considered by members in determining whether or not to provide specific services in individual circumstances. In some instances, they may represent an overall constraint on the nonaudit services that might be offered to a specific client. No hard-and-fast rules can be developed to help members reach these judgments, but they must be satisfied that they are meeting the spirit of the Principles in this regard.

In order to accomplish this, members should

- Practice in firms that have in place internal quality-control procedures to ensure that services are competently delivered and adequately supervised.
- Determine, in their individual judgments, whether the scope and nature of other services provided to an audit client would create a conflict of interest in the performance of the audit function for that client.
- Assess, in their individual judgments, whether an activity is consistent with their role as professionals (for example, is such activity a reasonable extension or variation of existing services offered by the member or others in the profession?).

Source: Excerpted from: AICPA *Code of Professional Conduct as Amended January 14, 1992.* Copyright © 1994 by the *American Institute of Certified Public Accountants, Inc.* Reprinted with permission.

The rules deal with issues such as the independence of members in the performance of their professional services; maintaining integrity and objectivity; the need to perform services competently and to comply with standards of practice, such as generally accepted accounting principles (GAAP) and generally accepted auditing standards (GAAS); keeping client information confidential; and adhering to guidelines that define acceptable practices related to advertising, forms or organization, and contingent fee and commission arrangements.

Management accountants have primary responsibility for financial reporting within an organization. They have a special duty to report financial information honestly and to safeguard company assets. Management accountants have an obligation to the organizations they serve, their profession, the public, and themselves to maintain the highest standards of ethical conduct. In recognition of these obligations, the Institute of Management Accountants (IMA) has promulgated four standards of ethical conduct for management accountants. They deal with professional competence in carrying out responsibilities, the confidentiality of information received during the course of work, the maintenance of integrity in carrying out duties, and the need for objectivity in communicating and disclosing all relevant information that could reasonably be expected to influence an intended user's understanding of the information. The IMA's *Standards of Ethical Conduct* appears in Exhibit 2 on pages 11–12.

Internal auditors function under the policies established by company management and the board of directors to monitor the performance of the organization's control systems and to help ensure the reliability and integrity of financial and operating information. The Institute of Internal Auditors (IIA) has established a code of ethics for its members that details the standards of proper professional conduct for internal auditors. The standards deal with the need for honesty, objectivity, and diligence in performing services; the need for loyalty; the need to avoid activities that create conflicts of interest in carrying out duties; the prohibition against accepting fees or gifts that might jeopardize the auditor's objectivity and that might conflict with the employee's interests; the need to exercise prudence in the use of confidential information; and the need to exercise due care to obtain sufficient factual evidence to support the expression of an opinion. The IIA's *Code of Ethics* appears in Exhibit 3 on pages 13–14.

The principle of objectivity embodied in the AICPA *Code of Professional Conduct* imposes the obligation to be impartial, intellectually honest, and free of conflicts of interest. The obligation of impartiality outlined in the AICPA Code goes beyond what is expected of management accountants and internal auditors, both of whom are expected to act in the employer's best interest within the bounds of honesty and integrity. Several cases in the book deal with situations where potential conflicts exist because of the need for objectivity in the performance of professional services and the need to best serve the interests of the organization. Some cases also deal with alternatives to whistle-blowing in situations containing present and potential improper activities.

The accounting environment has become increasingly complex and competitive over the past two decades. Advertising, direct solicitation of clients, the acceptance of commissions and contingent fees, and an expanding scope of professional services have all contributed to the rising level of complexity. At the same time, business transactions have become more varied and complex, and technical standards have proliferated. Public investors and others who rely on reported financial information have become increasingly concerned about instances of fraudulent financial reporting. In the current environment, accountants and auditors are faced with the challenge of maintaining their professionalism amidst increasing competition and other business pressures.

EXTERNAL ACCOUNTING ENVIRONMENT

The bankruptcy of several large, publicly owned companies during the early 1970s (such as Equity Funding, Penn Central, and National Student Marketing) turned the public's attention to the accounting profession. In particular, in its investigation of these and other bankruptcies, Congress asked, "Where were the auditors?" The House Subcommittee on Oversight and Investigations, chaired by Representative John E. Moss (D., Calif.), issued a report in 1976 calling for

EXHIBIT 2
Institute of Management Accountants
Standards of Ethical Conduct

Management accountants have an obligation to the organizations they service, their profession, the public, and themselves to maintain the highest standards of ethical conduct. In recognition of this obligation, the Institute of Management Accountants has promulgated the following standards of ethical conduct for management accountants. Adherence to these standards is integral to achieving the *Objectives of Management Accounting.** Management accountants shall not commit acts contrary to these standards nor shall they condone the commission of such acts by others within their organization.

Competence

Management accountants have a responsibility to:

- Maintain an appropriate level of professional competence by ongoing development of their knowledge and skills.
- Perform their professional duties in accordance with relevant laws, regulations, and technical standards.
- Prepare complete and clear reports and recommendations after appropriate analyses of relevant and reliable information.

Confidentiality

Management accountants have a responsibility to:

- Refrain from disclosing confidential information acquired in the course of their work except when authorized, unless legally obligated to do so.
- Inform subordinates as appropriate regarding the confidentiality of information acquired in the course of their work and monitor their activities to assure the maintenance of that confidentiality.
- Refrain from using or appearing to use confidential information acquired in the course of their work for unethical or illegal advantage either personally or through third parties.

Integrity

Management accountants have a responsibility to:

- Avoid actual or apparent conflicts of interest and advise all appropriate parties of any potential conflict.
- Refrain from engaging in any activity that would prejudice their ability to carry out their duties ethically.
- Refuse any gift, favor, or hospitality that would influence or would appear to influence their actions.

*Institute of Management Accountants. Statements on Management Accounting. Objectives of Management Accounting, Statement No. 1B, June 17, 1982.

(continued)

- Refrain from either actively or passively subverting the attainment of the organization's legitimate and ethical objectives.
- Recognize and communicate professional limitations or other constraints that would preclude responsible judgment or successful performance of an activity.
- Communicate unfavorable as well as favorable information and professional judgments or opinions.
- Refrain from engaging in or supporting any activity that would discredit the profession.

Objectivity

Management accountants have a responsibility to:

- Communicate information fairly and objectively.
- Disclose fully all relevant information that could reasonably be expected to influence an interested user's understanding of the reports, comments, and recommendations presented.

Resolution of Ethical Conflict

In applying the standards of ethical conduct, management accountants may encounter problems in identifying unethical behavior or in resolving an ethical conflict. When faced with significant ethical issues, management accountants should follow the established policies of the organization bearing on the resolution of such conflict. If these policies do not resolve the ethical conflict, management accountants should consider the following course of action:

- Discuss such problems with the immediate superior except when it appears that the superior is involved, in which case the problem should be presented initially to the next higher managerial level. If satisfactory resolution cannot be achieved when the problem is initially presented, submit the issues to the next higher managerial level.

If the immediate superior is the chief executive officer, or equivalent, the acceptable reviewing authority may be a group such as the audit committee, executive committee, board of directors, board of trustees, or owners. Contact with levels above the immediate superior should be initiated only with the superior's knowledge, assuming the superior is not involved.

- Clarify relevant concepts by confidential discussion with an objective advisor to obtain an understanding of possible courses of action.
- If the ethical conflict still exists after exhausting all levels of internal review, the management accountant may have no other recourse on significant matters than to resign from the organization and to submit an informative memorandum to an appropriate representative of the organization.

Except where legally prescribed, communication of such problems to authorities or individuals not employed or engaged by the organization is not considered appropriate.

EXHIBIT 3
The Institute of Internal Auditors
Code of Ethics

Purpose

A distinguishing mark of a profession is acceptance by its members of responsibility to the interests of those it serves. Members of the Institute of Internal Auditors (Members) and Certified Internal Auditors (CIAs) must maintain high standards of conduct in order to effectively discharge this responsibility. The Institute of Internal Auditors (Institute) adopts the *Code of Ethics* for Members and CIAs.

Applicability

This *Code of Ethics* is applicable to all Members and CIAs. Membership in The Institute and acceptance of the "Certified Internal Auditor" designation are voluntary actions. By acceptance, Members and CIAs assume an obligation of self-discipline above and beyond the requirements of laws and regulations.

The standards of conduct set forth in this *Code of Ethics* provide basic principles in the practice of internal auditing. Members and CIAs should realize that their individual judgment is required in the application of these principles.

CIAs shall use the "Certified Internal Auditor" designation with discretion and in a dignified manner, fully aware of what the designation denotes. The designation shall also be used in a manner consistent with all statutory requirements.

Members who are judged by the Board of Directors of The Institute to be in violation of the standards of conduct of the *Code of Ethics* shall be subject to forfeiture of their membership in The Institute. CIAs who are similarly judged also shall be subject to forfeiture of the "Certified Internal Auditor" designation.

Standards of Conduct

I. Members and CIAs shall exercise honesty, objectivity, and diligence in the performance of their duties and responsibilities.

II. Members and CIAs shall exhibit loyalty in all matters pertaining to the affairs of their organization or to whomever they may be rendering a service. However, Members and CIAs shall not knowingly be a party to any illegal or improper activity.

III. Members and CIAs shall not knowingly engage in acts or activities which are discreditable to the profession of internal auditing or to their organization.

IV. Members and CIAs shall refrain from entering into any activity which may be in conflict with the interest of their organization or which would prejudice their ability to carry out objectively their duties and responsibilities.

V. Members and CIAs shall not accept anything of value from an employee, client, customer, supplier, or business associate of their organization which would impair or be presumed to impair their professional judgment.

VI. Members and CIAs shall undertake only those services which they can reasonably expect to complete with professional competence.

(continued)

    VII. Members and CIAs shall adopt suitable means to comply with the *Standards for the Professional Practice of Internal Auditing.*

    VIII. Members and CIAs shall be prudent in the use of information acquired in the course of their duties. They shall not use confidential information for any personal gain nor in any manner which would be contrary to law or detrimental to the welfare of their organization.

    IX. Members and CIAs, when reporting on the results of their work, shall reveal all material facts known to them which, if not revealed, could either distort reports of operations under review or conceal unlawful practices.

    X. Members and CIAs shall continually strive for improvement in their proficiency, and in the effectiveness and quality of their service.

    XI. Members and CIAs, in the practice of their profession, shall be ever mindful of their obligation to maintain the high standards of competence, morality and dignity promulgated by The Institute. Members shall abide by the *Bylaws* and uphold the objectives of The Institute.

Accepted by Board of Directors July 1988

Source: Code of Ethics. Copyright © 1988 by the *Institute of Internal Auditors, Inc.* Reprinted with permission.

reform measures that would have increased the Securities and Exchange Commission's (SEC) role in regulating the accounting profession. The Senate Subcommittee on Reports, Accounting, and Management, chaired by Senator Lee Metcalf (D., Mont.), issued a report in 1977 that criticized the dominant position in the accounting profession of the then Big Eight firms. The report pointed to a lack of independence and the failure of the firms to adequately serve the public interest.

REPORTING IRREGULARITIES AND ILLEGAL ACTS

Congressional concern about the financial reporting process has increased in recent years because of a number of business failures. Representative John D. Dingell (D., Mich.), chair of the House Oversight and Investigations Subcommittee, which investigated business failures in 1985, has been a frequent critic of outside auditors of major companies for failing to blow the whistle on companies that fail to disclose business problems. Business failure cases such as those of Beverly Hills Savings and Loan and ESM Government Securities have led the subcommittee to conclude that these failures were really "audit failures."

    The quality of audit work continues to be scrutinized by Congress, in part because of the large number of failed savings and loan institutions. Critics charge that the financial losses of these institutions could have been sharply contained had auditors only blown the whistle sooner. At issue is the auditor's responsibility to disclose possible illegal acts on the part of a client. According to SAS

No. 53 and SAS No. 54, disclosure of irregularities and illegal acts to parties other than the client's senior management and its audit committee or board of directors is not ordinarily part of the auditor's responsibility. Furthermore, such disclosure would be precluded by an ethical or legal obligation of confidentiality unless the matter affects the auditor's opinion on the financial statements. The auditor is, however, obligated to report irregularities and illegal acts to the SEC under the disclosure requirements of Form 8-K if the auditor withdraws from the engagement because the board of directors has not taken appropriate remedial action.

The aforementioned Securities Reform Act of 1995 shortens the time within which illegal acts must be reported to the SEC. Under the new law, the board of directors has one business day to inform the SEC that the independent auditor reported a material illegal act and determined that senior management and the board either have not taken or are not expected to take appropriate action. If the auditor does not receive a copy of the board's report to the SEC within the one-business-day period, the auditor must resign from the engagement or furnish the SEC with a copy of the original fraud report.

THE EXPECTATION GAP

The independent auditor's responsibility is to audit and report on the financial statements that are prepared by management. Perceptions of shortcomings in the effectiveness of independent audits erode public confidence in the integrity of the financial reporting system. Concerns about the quality of financial reporting led the AICPA's Auditing Standards Board in 1988 to issue nine new standards. Those standards are designed to close the "expectation gap"—that is, the difference between what the public and the financial statement users perceive as the responsibilities of accountants and auditors and what accountants and auditors themselves see as their responsibilities.

Some of the requirements of the expectation gap standards have an effect on situations described in the cases. For example, SAS No. 55 broadens the scope of the auditor's responsibility to consider internal control when planning an audit. SAS No. 58 revises the auditor's standard report. SAS No. 59 requires the auditor to consider whether the aggregate results of all audit procedures performed during planning, performance, and evaluation indicate that there could be substantial doubt about the entity's ability to continue as a going concern for a "reasonable" period of time (not to exceed one year beyond the date of the audited financial statements). If the auditor concludes there is substantial doubt, then, according to SAS No. 58, an explanatory paragraph (following the opinion paragraph) describing that doubt should be included in the audit report. An example of the auditor's standard report (as required by SAS No. 58) and an example of an explanatory paragraph when there is substantial doubt about the company's ability to continue as a going concern (as required by SAS No. 59) are presented on the following pages.

The Standard Auditor's Report
Unqualified Opinion

We have audited the accompanying balance sheet of X Company as of December 31, 19XX, and the related statements of income, retained earnings, and cash flows for the year then ended. These financial statements are the responsibility of the company's management. Our responsibility is to express an opinion on these financial statements based on our audit.

We conducted our audit in accordance with generally accepted auditing standards. Those standards require that we plan and perform the audit to obtain reasonable assurance about whether the financial statements are free of material misstatement. An audit includes examining, on a test basis, evidence supporting the amounts and disclosures in the financial statements. An audit also includes assessing the accounting principles used and significant estimates made by management, as well as evaluating the overall financial statement presentation. We believe that our audit provides a reasonable basis for our opinion.

In our opinion, the financial statements referred to above present fairly, in all material respects, the financial position of X Company as of [at] December 31, 19XX, and the results of its operations and its cash flows for the year then ended in conformity with generally accepted accounting principles.*

[Signature]

[Date]

*"Reports on Audited Financial Statements," *Statement on Auditing Standards No. 58* (New York: AICPA, 1988).

Illustrative Required Paragraph When Substantial Doubt About the Company's Ability to Continue as a Going Concern Exists

The accompanying financial statements have been prepared assuming that the company will continue as a going concern. As discussed in note Z to the financial statements, the company has suffered recurring losses from operations and has a net capital deficiency that raises substantial doubt about the entity's ability to continue as a going concern. Management's plans in regard to these matters are also described in note Z. The financial statements do not include any adjustments that might result from the outcome of this uncertainty.*

*"The Auditor's Consideration of an Entity's Ability to Continue as a Going Concern," *Statement on Auditing Standards No. 59* (New York: AICPA, 1988).

In a recent survey of investor views of audit assurance, Epstein and Geiger found that the investing public holds auditors to a much higher level of accountability for detecting material misstatements as a result of *error* (unintentional misstatements) and as a result of *fraud* (intentional misstatements) than the profession had assumed.

The authors conclude that the profession's perception that an audit should provide only reasonable assurance of financial statement accuracy is held by a minority of investors. The majority of investors expect an audit to provide absolute assurance that the financial statements are free of all types of material misstatements. Thus, it appears that a gap still exists between auditors and investors on the level of assurance an audit provides. Epstein and Geiger believe that an important factor in closing this expectation gap is to increase auditors' sensitivity to management honesty and integrity (or lack thereof).[2]

COMMERCIALIZATION OF THE PROFESSION

There has been increasing concern in recent years about the commercialization of the accounting profession. Charges have been made by some in Congress that the profession, the CPA firms, and individual practitioners may be tempted to put business interests ahead of the longer-term public interest. These charges include two specific types of competitive excesses referred to as *low-balling* and *opinion shopping.*

The practice of low-balling consists of deliberately underbidding for an audit engagement not only in order to obtain an audit client but with the hope of securing more-lucrative management advisory or other consulting services from that client in the future. The possible danger is that the audit firm may cut costs on the engagement by decreasing staff time and by reducing or eliminating required audit procedures, and thereby sacrifice audit accuracy. The potential exists for CPAs to compromise their integrity and independence in such situations. Cases illustrating instances of low-balling are included in this book.

Some of the cases in this book deal with instances of opinion shopping—that is, a client's seeking out the views of various accountants until finding one that will go along with the client's desired—not necessarily most ethical—accounting treatment. In an effort to better identify this and other potential abuses surrounding a change of accountants, the SEC adopted measures to clarify and expand the disclosure requirements of Form 8-K, which must be filed with the SEC when there is such a change. The amended 8-K requires disclosures of whether a board of directors or audit committee discussed disagreements with the former accountants, whether the registrant company limited discussion of disagreements between new and former accountants, and whether the former accountants resigned or were dismissed.

INTERNAL ACCOUNTING ENVIRONMENT

The Treadway Commission report, cited earlier, placed primary responsibility for financial reporting on company management and directors. The Commission emphasized the importance of the ethical tone at the top, tight internal controls, strong accounting systems and personnel, an effective internal audit, and independent and diligent audit committees. The Commission stressed the importance of the role of

[2]Epstein, Marc J., and M. A. Geiger, "Investor Views of Audit Assurance: Recent Evidence of the Expectation Gap," *Journal of Accountancy,* January 1994, pp. 60–66.

the chief accounting officer, who generally has the primary responsibility for designing, implementing, and monitoring the company's financial reporting system and internal accounting controls. The chief accounting officer is in a sensitive position and may, in certain instances, be subject to a great deal of pressure imposed by members of top management as they attempt to manage earnings by changing or manipulating operating decisions or accounting methods. In extreme situations such as the Phar-Mor case, cited earlier, the CEO may expect the chief accounting officer to participate in fraudulent financial reporting. However, ethical and professional obligations require that the chief accounting officer take whatever action is necessary to prevent improper accounting and financial reporting.

Internal auditors are utilized by management to monitor the performance of the organization's control systems. Internal auditors also have a major role in the monitoring and enforcement of corporate codes of conduct. Additionally, internal auditors work with the independent public auditors in fulfilling the latter's obligation to audit the company's financial statements.

An effective internal audit function is an essential component of a favorable corporate ethical climate. In order to maintain objectivity, internal auditing must remain independent of the operations and decision-making processes of the organization. According to the Treadway Commission report, the internal audit function is most effective when the chief internal auditor reports administratively to a senior officer who is not directly responsible for preparing the company's financial statements. The chief internal auditor should have direct and unrestricted access to, and meet regularly with, both the chief executive officer and the audit committee of the board of directors.

THE CONTROL ENVIRONMENT

In 1992 the Committee of Sponsoring Organizations of the Treadway Commission (COSO) issued a report titled *Internal Control-Integrated Framework*. The report emphasizes the importance of the control environment to an ethical organizational environment. The control environment is one of five interrelated components of internal control. The other components are risk assessment, control activities, information and communication, and monitoring the internal control systems.

According to COSO, the control environment is the foundation for all other components of internal control. It sets the tone of the organization, influencing the control consciousness of its people. The control environment provides an atmosphere in which people conduct their activities and carry out their control responsibilities. One important element of the control environment is the integrity and ethical values of the people who create, administer, and monitor the internal controls. The integrity and ethical values of an organization reflect the commitment of the chief executive officer and the other members of top management to high ethical and behavioral standards. The Auditing Standards Board recently amended SAS No. 55 to incorporate COSO's definitions of the components of internal control, including that of the control environment.

WHISTLE-BLOWING

Internal accountants and auditors face on-the-job pressures that seriously test their commitment to perform objectively their responsibilities to protect the integrity of the financial reporting process within the company. Several of the cases in this book deal with instances of questionable accounting and reporting practices that create ethical dilemmas for these accountants and auditors. A common underlying theme of the cases is that industry accountants encounter situations that require them to make difficult decisions because of conflicts between loyalty considerations and the public interest.

Undoubtedly, the most difficult decision that a management accountant faces is whether to blow the whistle on financial wrongdoing. The IMA's ethical standards obligate management accountants to take whatever steps are necessary, *within* the organization, to resolve conflicts with superiors over financial reporting matters. The IMA does not, however, consider it to be appropriate for management accountants to go outside the organization and engage in external whistle-blowing.

In 1993 the AICPA issued *Interpretation 102-4* under Rule 102 in its Code. This pronouncement established specific actions that industry CPAs must take in order to avoid subordinating their professional judgment in violation of the integrity standard in the Code. There is general agreement between the IMA and the AICPA regarding the ethical obligations of management accountants when differences exist with superiors. In particular, the internal accountants are expected to take their concerns to higher levels in the organization so that the board of directors or the audit committee, or the owners of the business, have an opportunity to take corrective action. Both groups recommend that the accountants consider resigning from the entity if a material misstatement of the financial statements has gone uncorrected.

One difference between the AICPA and IMA guidelines is that the AICPA recommends that the industry accountant consider any obligations to the external auditors and regulatory authorities. Generally, the accountant should not contact regulatory authorities in violation of confidentiality, because there is no legal requirement to report an employer's criminal behavior. However, internal accountants may choose to go to the outside auditors early on because the external auditors are expected to work with the audit committee on such matters. The external auditors working with the audit committee should be able to resolve financial reporting conflicts in an ethically appropriate manner.

In summary, the profession's standards emphasize the confidentiality and loyalty obligations of accountants to their employers and clients in whistle-blowing situations instead of giving primary importance to the public's interest in having full disclosure of all the information that might reasonably be expected to influence the decisions of financial statement users. This emphasis has important implications for the ability of CPAs, CMAs, and CIAs to act in accordance with the profession's ethical norms of behavior. These norms are described in the section entitled "Philosophical Framework for Ethical Analysis."

FRAME OF REFERENCE FOR CASE ANALYSIS

Students are expected to analyze the facts of a case before responding to the questions posed at the end of each case. In many case situations there are no right or wrong answers. Instead, students should provide logical reasons for their answers in light of the facts and after considering the operating environment for the accounting professional. Students should develop their arguments by applying the accounting frame of reference, including the appropriate professional and ethical standards. The philosophical frame of reference that is described in the next section should also be used to guide the ethical analysis.

The questions raised at the end of each case do not specifically require students to use the ethical decision-making framework that is presented in the third section of the book ("Ethical Decision-Making Process"). Nevertheless, the elements of the framework should be used by students as guides in evaluating alternative courses of action by considering the sources of ethical obligation discussed in this first section of the book and in the next section.

PHILOSOPHICAL FRAMEWORK FOR ETHICAL ANALYSIS

There appear to be at least three situations that create ethical dilemmas for accounting professionals. First, the technical accounting or ethics rules may be unclear, thus requiring accountants to exercise moral judgment in applying the rules in specific situations. Second, there may be a conflict between the interests of the stakeholders. The *stakeholders* are those individuals and groups affected by the outcome of a decision. The stakeholders of the accounting profession are defined in the Public Interest Principle in the AICPA Code as "the clients, credit grantors, governments, employers, investors, the business and financial community, and others who rely on the objectivity and integrity of certified public accountants to maintain the orderly functioning of commerce." It is the "collective well-being" of these groups that defines the public interest. According to this principle, conflicts among stakeholders should be resolved by putting the interest of those members of the public other than clients and employers ahead of the interests of the latter two groups. A third type of ethical dilemma occurs when a conflict exists between the accountants' self-interest and what moral principles indicate ought to be done. The Integrity Principle in the AICPA Code cautions that "Service and the public trust should not be subordinated to personal gain and advantage."

Jim Gaa discusses the auditors' duties in stating that accountants should at least sometimes be willing to take an action that is against their own self-interest. Gaa refers to this as taking "the moral point of view."[1] Several cases in the book deal with situations that test the accountants' commitment to the moral point of view.

There are four sources of ethical obligation for accounting professionals. Each source should be considered as a possible constraint on decision making. One source is legal and regulatory requirements. Most social activities in the public and private sectors are regulated by extensive laws that establish obligations that may or may not have an ethical basis. The ethical principle of lawfulness imposes an ethical obligation to abide by laws simply because they are laws. An individual or organization caught violating even technical laws is generally regarded as unethical and, in addition to the civil and criminal penalties that may be invoked, lawbreaking often causes serious damage to the reputation of the organization and decision makers involved. The GAAP and GAAS rules previously referred to can be viewed as regulatory requirements because all state boards of accountancy expect licensed CPAs to follow these and other standards in the performance of professional services.

The accounting profession is governed by standards of conduct that supplement laws and impose additional ethical obligations on those in the profession. The standards of the primary accounting associations were discussed in the previous section, "Introduction."

A third source of ethical obligation is the specific standards of behavior established by organizations to supplement and extend laws and generally accepted professional practices. These standards are typically stated as credos, policies, or a code of conduct, or they may simply be established by an organizational culture. The results of a survey on ethics in business conducted by the Ethics Resource Center indicate the following: 60% of respondent corporations have a code of conduct; 33% provide ethics training programs for their employees; 33% have an ethics office or ethics ombudsman.[2]

The fourth source of ethical obligation is not unique to accounting professionals—or to any individual or group, for that matter. There are certain prescriptive moral standards that philosophers believe should be used to differentiate right from wrong in conflicting situations. These will be discussed in the two sections that follow "Ethical Analysis."

ETHICAL ANALYSIS

Ethical questions in business can be addressed at three different levels—the systemic (macro) level, the corporate level, and the individual (micro) level. The *systemic level* refers to the environment in which a business operates, including the economic, legal, social, and political institutions that affect the firm's operations.

---

[1]Gaa, James C., "The Auditor's Role: The Philosophy and Psychology of Independence and Objectivity," *Proceedings of the 1992 Deloitte and Touche/University of Kansas Symposium on Auditing Problems* (Lawrence: University of Kansas, 1992), pp. 7–43.

[2]Ethics Resource Center, *Ethics in American Business: Policies, Programs and Perceptions* (Washington, D.C.: Ethics Resource Center, Inc., 1994).

At this level, concerns are raised about the ethical rightness or wrongness of the system itself. Questions also arise about the just distribution of goods or services and the fairness of laws and government regulation.

A second level of analysis, the *corporate level,* is more specific and relevant to the cases in this book. Such analysis treats the company or firm as the basic unit. At this level concerns are raised about the ethical dimensions of decisions that affect the organization or those made by the organization that affect other institutions (such as government, labor, or the community as a whole). Questions arise about the effects that corporate structure and culture have on a firm's ability to make ethical decisions. One such question concerns the provisions of a corporate code of conduct and whether the lines of communication are sufficiently open to allow discussion of disagreements that may arise within an organization.

An example of a positive ethical climate is the response of Johnson & Johnson to two incidents of intentional Tylenol poisonings. The first occurred in 1982, and the second in 1986. One result of the first incident was that the company developed tamperproof packaging that is now the industry standard. After the second incident, management decided to withdraw from the market and no longer manufacture consumer capsule products. The cumulative effect of the two incidents was to create a one-time write-off against earnings of $140 million. The company subsequently recovered and gained a reputation as an ethical organization. Management's decision making during the Tylenol crisis was guided by the *Johnson & Johnson Credo.* This document details expected behavior in relationships with customers, employees, communities in which employees work and live, and stockholders. The *Johnson & Johnson Credo,* which follows on page 24, is much more than a corporate code of conduct. It establishes a philosophy for dealing with stakeholders that permeates all decision-making and corporate activities. It is an integral part of the corporate culture and symbolizes the ethical tone at Johnson & Johnson.

The third level of analysis, the *individual level,* applies to all of the cases in the book. It focuses on the role of the individual within the firm. Ethical analysis provides a systematic framework for dealing with the available alternative courses of action. Questions are raised that guide the analysis and help students to develop reasoning skills. Robert A. Cooke, in his essay entitled *Ethics in Business: A Perspective,* which was used in the Arthur Andersen Business Ethics Program, identifies four such questions, as follows:[3]

1. Does the action or anticipated action unfairly single out an individual or group?
2. Does the action or anticipated action violate the moral or legal rights of any individual or group?
3. Is the action or anticipated action in conformity with accepted moral standards?
4. Are there alternative courses of action that are less likely to cause harm?

[3]Cooke, Robert A., *Ethics in Business: A Perspective,* Arthur Andersen & Co., S.C., Business Ethics Program (1990).

Our Credo

We believe our first responsibility is to the doctors, nurses and patients,
to mothers and fathers and all others who use our products and services.
In meeting their needs everything we do must be of high quality.
We must constantly strive to reduce our costs
in order to maintain reasonable prices.
Customers' orders must be serviced promptly and accurately.
Our suppliers and distributors must have an opportunity
to make a fair profit.

We are responsible to our employees,
the men and women who work with us throughout the world.
Everyone must be considered as an individual.
We must respect their dignity and recognize their merit.
They must have a sense of security in their jobs.
Compensation must be fair and adequate,
and working conditions clean, orderly and safe.
We must be mindful of ways to help our employees fulfill
their family responsibilities.
Employees must feel free to make suggestions and complaints.
There must be equal opportunity for management,
and their actions must be just and ethical.

We are responsible to the communities in which we live and work
and to the world community as well.
We must be good citizens—support good works and charities
and bear our fair share of taxes.
We must encourage civic improvements and better health and education.
We must maintain in good order
the property we are privileged to use,
protecting the environment and natural resources.

Our final responsibility is to our stockholders.
Business must make a sound profit.
We must experiment with new ideas.
Research must be carried on, innovative programs developed
and mistakes paid for.
New equipment must be purchased, new facilities provided
and new products launched.
Reserves must be created to provide for adverse times.
When we operate according to these principles,
the stockholders should realize a fair return.

Johnson & Johnson

When addressing these questions, most ethicists believe that it is possible to make judgments about cultural norms and to establish moral standards that are universal. That is, ethics is not culturally relative, and most ethicists reject any claim that morality is relative to individual standards of conduct.

MORAL DEVELOPMENT AND VIRTUE

Ethical issues that arise in specific cases should be evaluated with reference to laws and regulatory requirements, applicable technical rules, and standards of professional conduct. In most situations the issues raised are not clear-cut and, therefore, students will have to go beyond the rules and standards in analyzing the ethical issues. The purpose of this section is to describe some of the commonly used reasoning methods and prescriptive moral standards that can guide the ethical analysis.

VIRTUES AND VALUES

Michael Josephson, the founder and executive director of the Josephson Institute of Ethics, believes that certain fundamental core values form the foundation of a healthy democratic society. Josephson identifies the following core ethical values: (1) *trustworthiness*, which includes honesty, integrity, promise keeping, and loyalty; (2) *respect*, which includes civility and tolerance; (3) *responsibility,* which includes accountability, diligence, and the pursuit of excellence; (4) *justice and fairness*, which include openness and impartiality; (5) *caring,* which includes kindness, compassion, and unselfishness; and (6) *civic virtue.* Josephson refers to these core values as *"the six pillars of character."*[4]

Since the actions that we take often affect others, the core ethical values reflect the characteristics of our behavior that concern moral duty. That is, they reflect what is right, good, or proper rather than what is pleasurable, useful, or desirable. The latter are personal values that may differ from one person to another, whereas ethical values are universal.

In his 1994 best-seller, *The Book of Virtues,* William Bennett identifies the ethical values as fundamental traits of character. Bennett refers to them as *virtues.* However, the author believes that ethical values become virtues over a period of time, as individuals internalize these qualities of behavior by practicing them and using them as standards to guide their actions and decisions.

VIRTUE THEORY

Virtue theory dates back to the ancient Greek philosophers, especially Plato and Aristotle. In writing about Aristotle's account of the virtues, Alasdair MacIntyre states that the exercise of virtue requires "a capacity to judge and to do the right

---

[4]"Youth Leaders Choose Core Language for Character Education," *Ethics: Easier Said Than Done,* issues 19 and 20 (Marina del Rey, CA: Josephson Institute of Ethics, 1992), pp. 65–81.

thing in the right place at the right time in the right way." Judgment is exercised not through a routinizable application of the rules, but as a function of possessing those dispositions that enable choices to be made about what is the good for people and by holding in check desires for something other than what will help to achieve this goal.[5]

MacIntyre relates virtues to the internal rewards of a practice. He differentiates between the *external rewards* of a practice (such as money, fame, and power) and the *internal rewards,* which relate to the intrinsic value of a particular practice. MacIntyre points out that every practice requires a certain kind of relationship between those who participate in it. The virtues are the standards of excellence that characterize relationships within the practice. To enter into a practice is to accept the authority of those standards, obedience to the rules, and the commitment to achieve the internal rewards. Some of the virtues that MacIntyre identifies are truthfulness and trust, justice, courage, and honesty.[6]

The accounting profession is a practice in the sense that MacIntyre discusses practices. The most important virtues for accounting professionals are those dispositional properties that enable accountants to meet their ethical obligations to clients, employers, and the public at large. For instance, in order for accountants to act objectively in performing professional services, such as auditing the financial statements of a client, they must have the inclination to be impartial and open-minded. That is, they must be committed to perform such services without bias and to avoid conflicts of interest. Impartiality is an essential virtue for judges in our judicial system. CPAs render judgment on the fairness of financial statements. Therefore, they should act impartially in carrying out their professional responsibilities.

Edmund Pincoffs believes that virtues (and vices) are dispositional properties that provide grounds for preference (or avoidance) of persons and, therefore, they can help us to decide with whom we want to enter into a relationship of trust.[7] For example, if honesty is a virtue, then a potential client who is honest would be preferred to one who is dishonest. If reliability and dependability are virtues, then a client who values these attributes would prefer to have an accountant with these traits of character rather than one who is unreliable and undependable. In the former case, the honest client is more likely to tell the truth and fully disclose relevant information that enhances the trust relationship between the external auditor and the client. In the latter case, a reliable and dependable accountant is more worthy of trust because that person is more likely to complete an engagement with due care and to maintain the confidentiality of client information.

Virtue considerations may have to be balanced in some situations. For exam-

[5]MacIntyre, Alasdair, *After Virtue* (Notre Dame, IN: University of Notre Dame Press, 1984), pp. 149–150.

[6]Ibid., pp. 187–192.

[7]Pincoffs, Edmund L., *Quandaries and Virtues* (Lawrence: University Press of Kansas, 1986), pp. 75–79.

ple, an employer expects the controller to be loyal, but the public trust demands that all relevant information be disclosed in the financial statements. If information that is potentially harmful to the employer's best interests (such as the existence of fraudulent financial transactions) comes to the attention of the controller, then the controller must weigh faithfulness to the employer and the duties of confidentiality and loyalty against the virtue of honesty and the fact that the public relies on the accuracy of the financial statement information for its decision making. Notwithstanding the accounting profession's admonition against external whistleblowing, the overriding moral obligation of the controller (and the external auditor) in this instance is to assure the disclosure of all information that the public has a right to know. The virtue of honesty enables these professionals to meet the expectations of the public.

There are limitations to loyalty. An employer may expect the controller to place the employer's interests so high that virtue is subordinated. Loyalty, however, is a reciprocal notion, and an employer has no right to ask the controller to sacrifice ethical principles in the name of a relationship of trust. Thus, although there is a duty of loyalty to one's employer (or client), it does not justify the violation of a virtue.[8]

The virtues enable accounting professionals to resolve conflicting duties and loyalties in a morally appropriate way. They provide accountants with the inner strength of character to withstand pressures that might otherwise overwhelm and negatively influence their professional judgment in a relationship of trust. The virtues are not independent of each other. Instead, the ability to exercise one virtue often will depend on the presence of another. For example, a person who lacks impartiality in performing professional services will not perform such services reliably.

In summary, virtue considerations apply both to the decision maker and to the act under consideration by that party. Virtue emphasizes the importance of certain qualities that define appropriate behavior and the right action to take. Many of the cases in the book deal with situations where the right action may be quite apparent, but the decision maker may not be inclined to do what it takes to carry out that action because of pressures that are imposed by employers or clients. The author has identified 11 virtues that enable accountants to fulfill their duties to employers, clients, and to the public interest. These are presented in Figure 1 on page 28.

MORAL DEVELOPMENT

An individual's ability to make reasoned judgments about moral matters develops in stages. The psychologist Lawrence Kohlberg concluded, on the basis of 20 years of research, that moral development occurs in a specific sequence of six stages

---

[8]Mintz, Steven M., "Virtue Ethics and Accounting Education," *Issues in Accounting Education,* Fall 1995, pp. 24, 31.

FIGURE 1
Virtue in Accounting

Duties	Code Requirements of the Accounting Profession	Enabling Virtues
Public Interest		
• Public trust	Integrity	Trustworthiness Benevolence Altruism
• Reliance on financial statements	Truthfulness Nondeception	Honesty Integrity
	Objectivity Independence	Impartiality Open-mindedness
Client/Employer		
• Performance of professional services	Loyalty (confidentiality)	Reliability Dependability Faithfulness
	Due care (competence and prudence)	Trustworthiness

Source: Mintz, Steven M., "Virtue Ethics and Accounting Education," *Issues in Accounting Education,* Fall 1995, p. 260. Reprinted with permission. American Accounting Association, 1995.

that may be divided into three levels of moral reasoning. Kohlberg's views on ethical development are helpful in understanding how individuals may internalize moral standards and, as they become more sophisticated in their use, apply them more critically to resolve conflict situations. A brief summary of Kohlberg's stages of moral development follows.[9]

Level 1—Preconventional

At the preconventional level (level 1), the individual is very self-centered. Rules are seen as something external imposed on the self.

[9]A more complete discussion can be found in two works by Lawrence Kohlberg: "Moral Stages and Moralization: The Cognitive Developmental Approach," in Thomas Lickona (ed.), *Moral Development and Behavior: Theory, Research, and Social Issues* (New York: Holt, Rinehart and Winston, 1976), and *Essays on Moral Development. Volume II, The Psychology of Moral Development* (New York: Harper and Collins, 1984).

Stage 1. At stage 1, an individual's actions are judged in terms of their physical consequences, such as the avoidance of punishment.

Stage 2. At stage 2, an individual is aware of other's needs, but satisfaction of the individual's own needs is the basic motivation for action.

Level 2—Conventional

At the conventional level (level 2), the individual is able to see situations from the point of view of a group, such as one's own family, peer group, or nation. Most adults fall into level 2, which has a member-of-society perspective.

Stage 3. At stage 3, an individual's actions are influenced by a desire to conform to group norms. The individual begins to consider how others view a situation, and conflicts are resolved through appeal to those norms.

Stage 4. At stage 4, an individual is concerned for order in society and preserving the rules of society. The individual looks to laws or rules for guidance in resolving conflict situations.

Level 3—Postconventional

At the postconventional level (level 3), the individual questions society's laws and values and redefines them in terms of moral principles that can be applied universally.

Stage 5. At stage 5, social contracts and mutual obligations are important. The individual is aware of potential conflicting views and opinions and emphasizes resolving the differences impartially and with due consideration of everyone's interests.

Stage 6. At stage 6, an individual's actions are based not so much on a system of laws but on universal moral and ethical principles that apply across all social classes and cultures. One example of such a moral principle is the golden rule ("Do unto others as you would have them do unto you"). The most important ethical principles deal with justice, equality, and the dignity of all people. If a law conflicts with an ethical principle, then an individual should act in accordance with the principle. An example of such an ethical principle is Kant's categorical imperative ("Act only as you would be willing that everyone should act in the same situation").

According to Kohlberg, people do not enter a later stage until they have passed through each of the earlier ones. Some people may never reach the later stages. Instead, they may remain stuck at one of the earlier stages throughout life.

Kohlberg's *justice orientation* is criticized by Dr. Carol Gilligan, who suggests that there is a second orientation that is overlooked by his theory. Gilligan identifies a *care-and-response orientation.* She claims that such an orientation is more central to female moral judgment and action than it is to male judgment and action. As such, understanding this different orientation is necessary in order to understand female moral judgment and action.

The developmental psychologist James Rest developed an instrument, the Defining Issues Test (DIT), that produces a measure of ethical reasoning known as the "P" score. The P score is interpreted as the relative importance the subject gives to principled moral considerations in making a moral decision. In other words, the P score is the percentage of a subject's postconventional (stages 5 and 6) thinking about what is right or wrong when faced with an ethical dilemma. Rest reports an association between the six stages and P score results, although the P score is not a substitute for assessment of progress through, or reasoning at, one of Kohlberg's stages of moral reasoning.[10]

The results of two recently published studies by accounting researchers indicate that CPAs reason primarily at stages 3 and 4. One possible implication of these results is that a large percentage of CPAs may be overly influenced by their relationship with peers, superiors, and clients (stage 3) or by rules (stage 4). Alternatively, many CPAs may be unable to critically apply the technical standards and rules of conduct (stage 5) when these requirements are unclear. Thus, a CPA who attempts to strictly apply the rules (stage 4) may be unable to do so and, as a result, that CPA is likely to be influenced by others in the decision-making process.[11]

Virtue considerations seem to exist at all stages of the conventional and postconventional levels. For example, at stage 3 a person is concerned about caring for others and maintaining trust in relationships. At stage 4 one's duties, as defined by the role one plays within a system (community), define what is right. At stage 5 the rights of others and consequences of actions (objective impartiality and due process considerations) take on increased prominence. Finally, at stage 6 right is defined by decisions of conscience based on justice principles.

ETHICAL REASONING METHODS

There are three commonly used methods to guide the analysis of ethical issues. They are (1) utilitarianism, (2) a rights-based approach, and (3) a justice-based approach. No one method is necessarily any better than another. Ethicists suggest that elements of each may be appropriate in dealing with ethical and moral dilemmas that, by their very nature, have no right or wrong answers. The methods are useful in providing a framework to analyze ethical issues and guide decision making.

[10]Rest, James R., *Development in Judging Moral Issues* (Minneapolis: University of Minnesota Press, 1979).

[11]Ponemon, Lawrence A., "Ethical Reasoning and Selection Socialization in Accounting," *Accounting, Organizations and Society* 17 (1992), pp. 239–258; and Shaub, Michael K., "An Analysis of the Association of Traditional Demographic Variables with the Moral Reasoning of Auditing Students and Auditors," *Journal of Accounting Education* (Winter 1994), pp. 1–26.

The basic elements of each of the methods are described below.[12] One method that is not discussed is "egoist theory." "Egoists," as the theory's adherents are called, believe that an act is moral when it advances the individual's long-term self-interest. This method is not consistent with the moral point of view in accounting.

UTILITARIAN THEORY

The utilitarian theory was first formulated in the eighteenth century by Jeremy Bentham and later refined by John Stuart Mill. *Utilitarians* look beyond self-interest to consider impartially the interests of all persons affected by an action. The theory emphasizes consequences of an action on the individuals affected by an action. Utilitarians recognize that trade-offs exist in decision making. The utilitarian is concerned with balancing social harms and benefits in order to reach a decision that maximizes net benefits and minimizes overall harms for all stakeholders.

Utilitarian philosophers are conventionally divided into two types, act-utilitarians and rule-utilitarians. An *act-utilitarian* is concerned with how a particular act in a particular situation will produce the greatest amount of utility. Little or no guidance is sought from rules or laws. According to this theory, the decision maker should evaluate the effect that alternative actions will have on all stakeholders and select the one that will result in the greatest good for the greatest number. In contrast, *rule-utilitarians* hold that rules have a central role in morality issues, a role that cannot be compromised by the demands of particular situations. For the rule-utilitarian, actions are justified by appeal to rules such as "Don't deceive," or "Don't bribe." According to the rule-utilitarian, an action is selected because it is required by the correct moral rules that everyone should follow. The correct moral rule is that which maximizes intrinsic value and minimizes intrinsic disvalue.

The utilitarian approach is common in certain types of business decisions, such as performance measurements and evaluations. However, as a tool of ethical analysis it suffers from the difficulty of measuring the potential costs and benefits of alternative actions. Also, determining the appropriate unit of analysis or measurement is a problem. That is, who are the relevant stakeholders—that is, those who are affected by a decision? Because actions by companies affect people in other countries, the relevant-stakeholder idea must have an international perspective. Utilitarian decision making also can lead to injustice, because the action that produces the greatest balance of value for the greatest number of people may bring

---

[12]For a more complete discussion of the ethical reasoning methods, see any one of the following business ethics textbooks: Beauchamp, Tom L., and N. E. Bowie, *Ethical Theory and Business,* 4th ed. (Englewood Cliffs, NJ: Prentice-Hall, 1993), Boatright, John R., *Ethics and the Conduct of Business* (Englewood Cliffs, NJ: Prentice-Hall, 1993), and Velasquez, Manuel G., *Business Ethics: Concepts and Cases,* 3d ed. (Englewood Cliffs, NJ: Prentice-Hall, 1992).

about unjustified harm or disvalue to a minority. However, the rule-utilitarian approach does have particular significance for accountants, who are expected to follow rules of professional conduct in carrying out their responsibilities.

THEORY OF RIGHTS

Formulations of *rights theories* first appeared in the seventeenth century in writings of Thomas Hobbes and John Locke. Modern rights theory is associated with the eighteenth-century philosopher Immanuel Kant. Rights theory assumes that individuals have certain entitlements that should be respected—such as freedom of speech and conscience, free consent, and the right to privacy and due process. All human beings possess these rights and the duty to respect them, regardless of any utilitarian benefits that the exercise of the rights and duties may provide for others. Unlike the utilitarian approach, in which morality is seen from the point of view of what is good for society as a whole, proponents of rights theory argue that moral standards should promote the individual's welfare and protect the individual's choices against encroachment by society.

Kant's theory establishes an individual's duty as a moral agent toward others who possess certain rights. It is based on a moral principle that he calls the *categorical imperative*. This principle requires that everyone should be treated as a free and equal person and proposes that everyone has a correlative duty to treat others in this way. According to the theory, an action is morally correct if it is motivated by a sense of obligation and not because an action may be taken merely to advance one's personal interests. One version of Kant's categorical imperative emphasizes the universality of moral actions. The principle is stated as follows: "I ought never to act except in such a way that I can also will that my maxim (reason for acting) should become a universal law." According to this perspective, the morality of an action should be evaluated based on whether everyone would act this way in a similar situation for similar reasons.

A decision maker who advocates a rights approach should take an action only if it does not violate the rights of any stakeholders. Although this is an attractive approach to moral reasoning, rights theory sometimes can be difficult to implement, because of the need to balance conflicting rights.

The theory of rights holds particular importance for accountants since they have a public interest obligation. Moreover, when stakeholders' interests conflict, the accountant should be guided by the moral point of view. That is, the public interest should be given priority over the interest of others (such as a client, an employer, or one's self).

THEORY OF JUSTICE

Formulations of *justice theories* date back to Aristotle and Plato in the fifth century B.C. An important modern contributor to the theory of justice is John Rawls. The major components of justice theory are equity, fairness, and impartiality. These concepts require that actions taken reflect comparative treatment of individuals and groups affected by the action. Questions of *distributive justice* arise when conflicts of interest exist over the fair distribution of goods and services. The fundamental principle of distributive justice is that equals should be treated equally, and unequals, unequally. That is, those with an equal claim to resources should be treated the same, while those with a greater (or lesser) claim should receive a larger (or smaller) share of the resources. The theory is relevant for accountants since professional and ethical standards require them to be unbiased and consistent in making judgments.

In a business context, justice theory stipulates that the right decisions to be made are those that lead to a fair and equitable allocation of resources among the stakeholders. The theory of justice can be difficult to apply in practice, however, especially when the rights of some may have to be sacrificed in order to ensure a somewhat better distribution of benefits to others. For example, the president of a company may decide to allocate a larger share of the resources than seems to be justified to a division that is experiencing difficulty in becoming profitable in order to help promote its operations.

Individually, utilitarian theory, the theory of rights, and the theory of justice provide a framework for ethical analysis that can be useful in resolving ethical dilemmas. Elements of each reasoning approach should be considered, along with virtue theory, in selecting an appropriate course of action in the ethics case situations presented in this book. The next section of the book presents a decision-making process that provides structure to the analysis of ethical issues that arise in the cases. A case situation is then presented to illustrate the application of the process.

ETHICAL DECISION-MAKING PROCESS

A decision-making process can help to organize the various elements of ethical decision making discussed in the first two sections of the book. The framework below is recommended because it incorporates all sources of ethical obligation and provides a practical check on the ethical propriety of decisions.

1. Determine the Facts.   Specify the relevant facts, including differences of opinion, disagreements, and other conflict situations.

2. Identify the Operational Issues.   Determine the operational and behavioral issues.

3. Identify the Accounting Issues.   Decide which accounting concepts, accounting principles, and financial reporting practices are in question.

4. Identify the Stakeholders and Obligations.   Determine the duties and responsibilities of the accountants to each of the stakeholders who will be affected by the decision.

5. Make an Ethical Analysis of the Alternatives.   For each alternative, determine the following:

- Is it legal?
- Is it consistent with professional standards?
- Is it consistent with in-house rules?
- Is it right?

- Is it fair?
- Is it beneficial?
- Is it consistent with virtue considerations?

6. Decide on a Course of Action.   After evaluating the alternatives, the decision maker should eliminate unethical options and select the best ethical alternative.

7. Double-Check Your Decision—Question It.   Ask yourself these questions:

> "How would I feel if my decision were printed in the local newspaper?"
> "How would I feel if my family were to find out about my decision?"

The final step in the decision-making process is one that Michael Josephson, the director of the Josephson Institute of Ethics, recommends as a check on the analysis. It is designed to determine whether the decision maker has internalized the ethical norms. In other words, the decision maker should feel confident about explaining or defending the basis for the decision because it conforms with all of the ethical requirements.

The questions that are raised at the end of each case do not always require students to go through all the steps in the decision-making process. Many of the cases are followed by specific questions that are designed to have students apply only selected methods of ethical analysis. This approach enhances the diversity of case experiences for students. In these and other situations, students should use the various elements of the process as a guide to ensure that all relevant professional and ethical issues have been considered in responding to the questions.

ILLUSTRATION OF CASE ANALYSIS—QUESTRONICS

The following case situation has been developed to illustrate the application of ethical analysis using the seven-step decision-making process. The issues presented in this case are uncomplicated ones, unlike most of those dealt with in the cases in the book. Here, the focus is on explaining how to apply the decision-making process.

CASE SITUATION

Questronics was formed in March 1994 with the goal of developing and marketing a word processing software package that could revolutionize the way that text material was edited and formatted prior to printing the final copy. As a start-up enterprise, Questronics received $2 million in venture capital during 1994 from two private investors, Tom Howe and Bill Stephens. These funds were expected to run out by the end of 1995. Questronics had not lined up additional financing by the time that the audit was completed on the December 31, 1994, financial statements. Therefore, the audit report of Hart and Spencer contained an explanatory paragraph describing the substantial doubt that existed with respect to Questronics's ability to continue as a going concern.

During 1995 Questronics began to receive advance orders for delivery in 1996 of its software product. Orders in the amount of $200,000 were received. However, the $2 million of initial venture capital ran out at the end of 1995, and additional funds were still needed in order to complete product development. Tom Howe and Bill Stephens expressed an interest in continued financing of Questronics's operations. However, they were concerned that competitors might come out with similar software products before Questronics did. Howe and Stephens delayed a final decision on financing until they received audited financial statements for the year ended December 31, 1995.

The audit of the December 31, 1995, financial statements revealed a $500,000 revenue item for a sale to Groth Industries. Upon investigation, Ed Wells, the accountant in charge of the Questronics audit, discovered that Questronics had negotiated a contract with Groth Industries for the sale of 50,000 word processing packages to be delivered in August 1996. Prior to signing the $5 million contract, Groth Industries backed out, stating that it wanted to reconsider alternatives to acquiring a new word processing package. Questronics threatened litigation against Groth Industries but eventually accepted a $500,000 "apology" payment in lieu of taking legal action. Questronics recorded this amount as revenue.

Ed Wells requests a meeting with Paul Francis, the controller, and Jack Daly, the president of Questronics. At the meeting Wells points out that the $500,000 should have been included in miscellaneous ("other") income, because the payment was not for the sale of Questronics's product in the normal course of business. Francis and Daly explain that it is important to include the $500,000 in revenue in order to favorably impress Howe and Stephens. Francis and Daly insist that the key to securing needed funds from Howe and Stephens is to make it appear that Questronics is earning revenue from the sale of its product. They point out that it will take time to identify alternative sources of financing if funding is not forthcoming from Howe and Stephens.

Ed Wells knows that if Questronics is successful in its current round of financing, then it will likely complete product development by mid-1996 and begin to show profitable operations by year-end. Wells also knows that Questronics plans to go public in two or three years. He does not want to take any action that might jeopardize his firm's position with respect to current and future audit work and other services that might be rendered for Questronics. Wells thinks that, although the $500,000 does not qualify as revenue from the sale of a product, this amount is part of the company's 1995 income and, perhaps, little harm will be done by keeping it in the revenue category rather than reclassifying it as "other income."

APPLICATION OF DECISION-MAKING PROCESS

1. Facts

- The $2 million in start-up funds received from Howe and Stephens ran out in 1995.
- An audit report on the December 31, 1994, financial statements contained an explanatory paragraph describing the substantial doubt that existed with respect to Questronics's ability to continue as a going concern.
- Advance orders of $200,000 were received in 1995.
- Additional funds are needed to complete product development. Howe and Stephens are potential sources, but they first want to see the audited statements for December 31, 1995.
- Ed Wells questions treatment as operating revenue the $500,000 apology payment by Groth Industries for backing out of the contract.
- Wells meets with Daly (president) and Francis (controller). He points out that the $500,000 is a nonoperating item that should be reclassified into an account that clearly depicts the payment as other income.
- Daly and Francis express their concerns that Questronics must be perceived as earning revenue from its operations if it is to secure needed funds from Howe and Stephens.
- Wells knows that successful financing for Questronics will likely lead to profitable operations by the end of 1996.
- Questronics may go public in two or three years. Therefore, Wells is concerned about losing a potentially lucrative client if he takes a firm stand on the revenue matter.

2. Operational Issues

- The internal control system is not operating as it should. The $500,000 should have been recorded as other income. Management override of internal controls may explain the situation.
- The integrity of top management is an issue, and the culture of the organization may foster additional intentional misstatements in the future. The tone at the top is not a very ethical one.
- Wells should be concerned that Francis condones the improper accounting. He must be able to rely on the work of Francis and others involved in the financial reporting system.
- If Wells does not support the company's position, it could delay product development and even threaten the continued existence of Questronics.
- If Wells goes along with the company's position, the result may be successful product development and profitability. If, however, the product is not marketed successfully, then the investors may lose their investment and file lawsuits against the company and its outside auditors.

3. Accounting Issues

- Accountants are expected to maintain objectivity and not to subordinate their judgment to that of the client.
- The $500,000 revenue treatment is not in conformity with generally accepted accounting principles (GAAP). The audit firm should not render an unqualified opinion on the Questronics financial statements, because there is a material departure from GAAP.
- Client-retention concerns should not be given priority over the public's need for accurate and reliable financial statements.

4. Stakeholders and Obligations

- *Questronics and Top Management.* These stakeholders should expect the auditors to carry out their responsibilities in a reliable and dependable manner and to demonstrate faithfulness by maintaining the confidentiality of company information. Daly and Francis seem to support a less ethical responsibility, that is, they want the auditors to go along with the company's treatment of the $500,000.
- *Howe and Stephens and Other Potential Investors.* The investors will rely on the financial statement information in deciding whether to provide additional financing for the company. The investors expect the auditors to be honest and trustworthy.
- *Wells and the Audit Firm.* The auditors are stakeholders. They have an ethical obligation to honor the public trust and maintain their own integrity. If the auditors go along with Daly and Francis, then the audit firm stands to gain additional business in the future. Therefore, pressure may be imposed by the firm on Wells, and his loyalty to the organization may be tested.
- *Regulatory Authorities.* If Questronics does go public in two or three years, then the SEC becomes a stakeholder, because the statements for the year ended December 31, 1995, probably will be included in the initial registration filing.

5. Ethical Analysis of the Alternatives
Alternative A: Go along with the company's accounting for the $500,000.

- *Legality.* GAAP is violated: revenue-recognition principles require that items classified as operating income should be earned in the normal and ordinary course of business.
- *Professional Standards.* Wells violates the integrity standard (Rule 102) in the AICPA Code, because he has subordinated his judgment to that of the client. Wells also violates the GAAP rule (Rule 203), because he should not give an unqualified opinion when there is a material departure from GAAP.
- *In-House Rules.* No information is provided about the audit firm's internal

code of conduct, although it is difficult to imagine that the firm would sanction the subordination of professional judgment in such a clear-cut situation.

- *Rights Theory.* The rights of Howe and Stephens are violated. These investors have a right to receive accurate and reliable financial information prior to making a decision on additional funding for Questronics. The auditors have an obligation to ensure that the statements are not materially misstated. Any attempt to deliberately misstate the financial statements is inconsistent with the intent of Kant's categorical imperative.

- *Justice Theory.* Wells is biased in sanctioning the company's position instead of insisting on proper accounting procedures. It is not fair to Howe and Stephens—and other potential investors—to emphasize client-retention issues over proper accounting. The financial statements will not contain a fair presentation of the financial information.

- *Utilitarian Theory.* Wells rationalizes that going along with the client is acceptable because Questronics may be harmed if it is not able to secure additional funding. The auditors can benefit, at least in the short run, by going along with the client because, by doing so, it may receive additional business in the future. However, the client may consequently expect the auditors to go along with its position when other matters arise in the future where there is a difference of opinion on a GAAP issue. Harm may come to the auditors if they sanction the improper revenue treatment and Questronics goes public, because the SEC will then question the accounting procedure.

- *Virtue Theory.* *Honesty* requires that the statements disclose all relevant information that the users need for their decision making. The statements should not mislead Howe and Stephens by creating the false impression that Questronics is earning a significant amount of money from operating activities. *Impartiality* necessitates that Wells not be biased by client-retention issues and be fair-minded about the need for accurate and *reliable* financial statements. *Trustworthiness* requires that Wells and the audit firm not violate the faith that investors have in the auditors—specifically, the belief that they will support the need for truthful financial statement information. *Integrity* requires that Wells not give in to the pressures imposed by the client and, perhaps, the audit firm, to go along with the improper recording of the $500,000. Wells needs to have the moral courage to withstand such pressures, even if doing so results in loss of the client or the loss of his job.

Alternative B: Refuse to go along with the GAAP departure, and withdraw from the engagement, if necessary.

This is the desired course of action, because the auditors do not want to be put in a position of sanctioning GAAP violations and violating the profession's standards of ethical behavior. An important point is that it is not truly in Questronics's best interest to produce false and misleading financial statements. Daly and Francis may believe that it is in the best interests of the company to do so, but in reality they mean it is potentially in their best interests. They could be rewarded if the company is successful in securing additional financing and operations become profitable as a result of their conduct. Moreover, the moral point of view requires that Wells put the public interest and the interests of Howe and Stephens ahead of self-interest and of the interests of his employer, assuming the audit firm goes along with Questronics. In other words, Wells should not give priority to the external rewards of accounting practice. Instead, he should focus on the internal rewards of the profession. That is, he should seek to facilitate the fair presentation of financial information that can be relied upon by investors and other users for their decision-making needs. He thereby helps to facilitate the efficient allocation of economic resources in our economy.

6 and 7. Decision and Check

As stated above, Wells should refuse to sanction the improper accounting, even if he must therefore withdraw from the engagement. Wells should be proud of the decision. It is consistent with his ethical obligations, and it is the morally appropriate decision in this case.

ETHICAL ANALYSIS

A useful tool of ethical analysis is to develop a *decision tree*. A decision tree helps in analyzing the possible implications of alternative courses of action. It is especially helpful in utilitarian analysis, because it focuses attention on the consequences of alternative actions. Figure 1 illustrates how such a decision tree might look.

FIGURE 1
Decision Tree Analysis

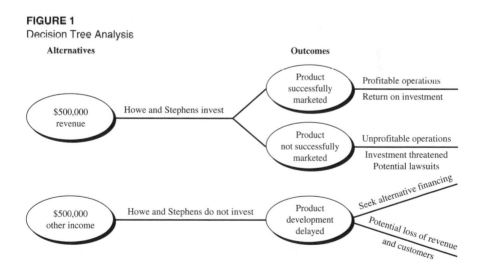

CASES

HUMAN RESOURCE ISSUES

Ethical Considerations in Making Human Resource Decisions

∎

BACKGROUND

Ethical issues arise in a variety of human resource situations. For example, the employees of an organization should be treated fairly and not discriminated against—regardless of age, sex, race, or disability. In their performance of professional services, accountants can face discrimination on the basis of any one of these factors. However, this section focuses on issues that may be faced by accounting graduates early in their careers, especially those that deal with interpersonal relationships. Some of the issues are as follows:

- Character traits important in performing professional services in a competent and objective manner
- Gender issues that an employer must deal with, such as family leave or commitments, flexible time schedules, and retention of women who go on extended maternity leave
- Employer policies regarding employee dating and employee relationships with suppliers, customers, and client entities
- Potential conflicts of interest faced by an employer that may affect employee performance and client service
- Employer's expectations of employees and performance evaluation systems that take these factors into consideration

Human resource issues have an important ethical component. For example, a performance evaluation system should include clear and consistent expectations, and it should be fairly administered. All employees should be treated equally by an organization, regardless of their gender, age, race, or religion. However, it is possible to argue under the justice theory that this is not always the case. For example, under the justice theory it can be argued that, because of gender-determined factors such as child bearing and family responsibilities, women and men are not equal. The question then is, Should an organization provide certain benefits to women (or men) that are not provided to the other group in order to accommodate family commitments? Human resource considerations related to women in the accounting profession are explored in the first case in this section.

SOCIALIZATION IN THE ACCOUNTING PROFESSION

The results of two surveys indicate that accounting graduates should be aware that recruiters in the profession look for values such as honesty, reliability, trustworthiness, and a willingness to honor the public trust and public interest. These and other qualities of ethical behavior ranked higher than most other characteristics sought in entry-level accountants by various employers of accounting graduates. They included factors such as communication skills and accounting education and knowledge.[1]

An interesting finding of the surveys is that accounting recruiters rank "congeniality characteristics" higher than they do factors such as accounting education and knowledge, work experience, and academic achievement. If these results accurately reflect the consensus of recruiters in the accounting profession, then students need to pay attention to developing traits such as friendliness, good manners, and a sense of humor. These traits enable an accountant to get along with clients, customers, and colleagues, and to be accepted by the latter group. Moreover, factors such as one's personal problems, maturity level, appearance, and personal disposition were all ranked higher than the aforementioned congeniality characteristics. Each of these factors also affects how we get along with others and whether we are accepted by them.

Accounting students who are planning to enter the accounting profession should become familiar with the profession's expectations regarding employee conduct. In particular, there are certain traits of character that are important to the development of trust in the professional relationships that exist in accounting and that are an integral part of the profession's socialization process. For example, trustworthiness is a trait of character that inspires confidence on the part of those who rely on the good intentions of others to perform services competently and in their best interests. An accountant who is honest can be expected (that is, trusted) to fully disclose all the information necessary to assure that the financial statements are

[1]Ahadiat, Nasrollah, and K. J. Smith, "A Factor-Analytic Investigation of Employee Selection Factors of Significance to Recruiters of Entry-Level Accountants," *Issues in Accounting Education,* Spring 1994, pp. 59–79; and Ahadiat, Nasrollah, and J. J. Mackie, "Ethics Education in Accounting: An Investigation of the Importance of Ethics as a Factor in the Recruiting Decisions of Public Accounting Firms," *Journal of Accounting Education,* Fall 1993, pp. 243–257.

not misleading. However, it is the virtue of integrity that ensures that the accountant will not subordinate honesty to the loyalty demands of an employer or client.

TRAITS OF CHARACTER AND ETHICAL BEHAVIOR

Recall that virtues are dispositional properties that provide grounds for preference (or avoidance) of persons. Therefore, they can help us to decide with whom do we want to enter into a relationship of trust. For example, if reliability and dependability are virtues, then a client who values these attributes would prefer to have an accountant with these traits of character rather than one who is unreliable and undependable. A reliable and dependable accountant is more worthy of trust, because that person is more likely to complete an engagement with due care and maintain the confidentiality of client information.

Virtue provides the link between possessing certain traits of character and being able to act ethically. In other words, a virtuous person—that is, one who has internalized admirable traits of character—acts in a certain way (or avoids acting in other ways) out of the knowledge that it is the right way to behave, and not necessarily for reasons related to self-interest. Thus, virtue enables accountants to act responsibly in dealing with other employees and members of top management and to satisfy their public interest obligations.

APPLICATION OF ETHICAL REASONING TO HUMAN RESOURCE DECISIONS

Human resource issues have an ethical component. They focus on how an organization treats its employees and how employees treat each other. The golden rule establishes the standard that we should treat others the way we want to be treated. For example, I would not want to have a fellow employee lie or deceive others about my performance, therefore I should not do these things to others. The theory of rights, which is similar to the golden rule, requires that I should act only in ways that I am willing to have others act for similar reasons in similar situations. Kant's principle of universality can be illustrated as follows: I do not take credit for the work of others and would not want others to receive credit for my work. What if everyone falsely received credit for work that they did not do?

One aspect of the theory of justice is that scarce resources should be allocated in a fair and just way. For example, if I am the manager of one of many departments in a company, then I should be concerned about the fairness of resource allocations to my department. Moreover, I want to receive a just share of the bonus payments and other incentives based on a fair performance evaluation system.

Utilitarian decisions are quite common in business. The utilitarian method of reasoning is similar to cost-benefit analysis. According to utilitarian reasoning, as noted earlier, the right action to take is the one that produces the greatest net benefits to all of the stakeholder groups affected by an action. For example, let us assume that it is possible to measure the costs and benefits of a decision regarding whether to provide free child-care facilities at the office for employees or to require that employees undertake this responsibility on their own. Then, a decision based on utilitarian considerations can be made as to whether to provide these facilities. Of course, one problem is to accurately measure factors such as increased efficiency when child care is provided due to less frequent absences by employees who would otherwise have to care for their children at home.

CONCLUSION

Employees are the most important resource for any organization. The qualities that each employee brings to a job can significantly affect both the employee's performance and that of the organization. Relations inside the organization reflect how employees treat each other and how the organization treats its employees. The ultimate success of an organization may depend on whether members of top management establish policies that are fair to employees and that help to foster efficient and effective performance. Accounting students need to know how to evaluate human resource situations, because these are some of the very first issues they will confront in the accounting profession. Hopefully, the cases that follow will help to sensitize students to some of these issues and to the importance of ethical behavior in dealing with them.

Helen Alyon

■

WOMEN IN THE ACCOUNTING PROFESSION

The gender mix in the accounting profession has changed dramatically since the 1970s. Back then, a significant majority of the bachelor's degrees in accounting were awarded to males. By 1994 there was a reversal in the gender mix so that 54% of the bachelor's degrees in accounting were awarded to females. Although males still receive more master's and doctoral degrees than do females (57% and 66%, respectively, are awarded to males), the trend is toward a higher percentage of female recipients for these degrees as well. Women have been entering the public accounting profession in substantial numbers over the last 25 years. In fact, 50% of new graduates hired by CPA firms in 1994 were female.[2] However, a 1993 study found that, on average, only 12% of the partners were female. The percentage varies from 6% for firms with more than 200 staff to 15% for firms with fewer than 21 staff members. Perhaps the good news is that the average number of new female partners in all firms in 1993 was 26%, with the percentage varying from 13% to 39% for the larger and smaller firms, respectively. The bad news is that a larger percentage of females than males leave public accounting, especially at the supervisory and senior levels.[3]

The results of a 1993 study of the stress felt by women in public accounting indicate that female accountants experience higher levels of job-related tension than do their male counterparts. The findings also indicate that stress is more important in the decision to leave public accounting for women than for men. The reasons for the greater levels of stress among women include the heavy time demands of the profession, difficulty balancing home and work commitments, and greater likelihood of having an unfulfilling job or of lacking career advancement opportunities.[4]

[2] *The Supply of Accounting Graduates and the Demand for Public Accounting Recruits—1995,* American Institute of Certified Public Accountants (AICPA).
[3] *Women's Status and Work/Family Initiatives in Public Accounting,* August 1994, AICPA.
[4] Collins, Karen M., "Stress and Departures from the Public Accounting Profession: A Study of Gender Differences," *Accounting Horizons,* March 1993, pp. 29–38.

One of the challenges faced by the accounting profession is how to retain women in the profession. This is important because of the increasing number of female graduates and the need to attract the "best and brightest" to the profession. The American Institute of CPAs (AICPA) has been addressing the issue of women's upward mobility since 1984, when it formed a committee to study the obstacles to mobility and recommend measures for overcoming these obstacles. The seven biggest obstacles to mobility were identified as (1) cultural attitudes about women in the workplace; (2) the perception of some employers that there are no gender-related obstacles, which could be frustrating to women—who know better; (3) the lack of awareness of some women of the commitment needed to advance as a woman in an organization; (4) the assumption of some employers that child-care and family responsibilities will take priority over the needs of the organization; (5) dealing with the added stress of balancing career and family interests; (6) discrimination against women who become emotionally involved with male employees; and (7) lack of women's participation in professional associations and industry organizations.

The case that follows illustrates one aspect of the problem for the public accounting profession. The issue here is whether a CPA firm can make the necessary concessions to retain competent women without appearing to favor females over their male counterparts.

CASE SITUATION

Helen Alyon has worked for Brownwood & Short LLP for eight years. Alyon was recently promoted to manager, and she appears to be on a "fast track" to becoming only the third female partner of the international CPA firm. Alyon is a real go-getter and is liked by everyone in the firm. Nine months ago Alyon asked for and received a six-month maternity leave of absence without pay. It is standard practice for the firm to approve such leaves for women (or for men who ask for paternity leave).

At the time Alyon asked for the leave she was adamant about her intention to return to work on a full-time basis. However, after spending six months bonding with her newborn daughter, Alyon decided to request a reduced workload. She knows that other women have been allowed to cut back to half-time under similar circumstances. Alyon assumes that her request will be approved as well.

Alyon meets with her mentor, Lester Parsons, to discuss the firm's position on the change in her employment status. Parsons tells Alyon that her future is a bright one, but that her progress toward partnership will be affected if she goes on half-time status. For one thing, she will not be able to service as many clients as do the full-time managers. For another, she will not be available to clients five days a week, in direct violation of the firm's policy. While the firm might be willing to put her on a delayed partnership track for as long as three years, it cannot agree to do so for longer than that. Parsons cautions Alyon that, even if she returns to full-time status after three years, the possibility exists that she will not be as highly thought of then as she is now. Some may question her commitment to the profession and to doing what it takes to "help grow" the business. This is a critical component in partnership decisions by the firm.

Alyon is a bit surprised by the reaction of her mentor. She does not object to the candid advice, but Parsons's demeanor is not as cordial as in the past. She wonders whether his words of warning are more an expression of the way things are at the firm. Maybe the other managers and the partners would be jealous if the firm were to treat her differently by allowing her to work half-time for three years and still be on a partnership track. Perhaps this is why the female partners both returned to work full-time after a six-month maternity leave.

Parsons suggests that Alyon consider the matter in light of their discussion and that the two of them meet again on Monday morning.

QUESTIONS

1. Describe the ethical issues that exist for an accounting firm such as Brownwood & Short in establishing a human resource policy for women who want to work less than full-time because of family commitments. Based on the limited facts of this case, do you think the firm of Brownwood & Short has a policy that is consistent with the ethical treatment of its employees?
2. Assume that Alyon asks Parsons to work at home two days a week, where she can transmit memos to the office from her home computer using a modem, and to come into the office or be at a client's office the other three days a week. What are the issues that should be of concern to Parsons and the firm in deciding whether to grant Alyon's request?

Ed Giles and Susan Regas

■

Ed Giles and Susan Regas have never been happier than during the past four months, since they have been dating each other. Giles is a 35-year-old CPA and a partner in the medium-sized accounting firm of Saduga & Mihca. Regas is a 25-year-old senior in the same firm. Both Giles and Regas know the firm's policy on dating. Although it is acceptable for peers to date, the firm does not permit two members of different ranks within the firm to date. A partner should not date a senior in the firm anymore than a senior should date a junior staff accountant. If such dating eventually leads to marriage, then one of the two must resign because of the conflict of interests. Giles and Regas have tried to be discreet about their relationship because they don't want to create any suspicions.

While most of the staff seem to know about Giles and Regas, it is not common knowledge among the partners that the two of them are dating. Perhaps that is why Regas was assigned to work on the audit of CAA Industries for a second year, even though Giles is the supervising partner on the engagement.

As the audit progresses, it becomes clear to the junior staff members that Giles and Regas are spending personal time together during the workday. On one occasion they were observed leaving for lunch together. Regas did not return to the client's office that day until three hours later. On another occasion Regas seemed distracted from her work, and later that day she received a dozen roses from Giles. A friend of Regas's, Ruth Revilo, inadvertently discovered this fact when she happened to see the card that accompanied the flowers.

Revilo asks to speak with Regas after the other staff members leave for the day. She tells Regas that she is not the only staff member on the audit who knows about the relationship between Giles and Regas. Revilo cautions Regas about jeopardizing her future with the firm by getting involved in a serious dating relationship with someone of a higher rank. Regas does not respond to this comment. Instead, she admits to being distracted lately because of an argument she had with Giles. She points out that the flowers are his way of saying he is sorry for some of the things that were said. Regas confides in Revilo that she was upset by a statement Giles made in response to the problem Regas was having lately in getting to work on time. Regas suggested that it might be best if they did not go out during the workweek. Giles was upset by this suggestion. He emphasized the importance of their relationship to him. But, then, in a moment of anger he said to Regas: "I've put everything on the line for you. There's no turning back for me."

The discussion between Regas and Revilo ends after Regas promises to talk to Giles about the effect their relationship is having on her job performance. Regas concludes by telling Revilo that she wants to continue her relationship with Giles, but that she does not want to jeopardize her future with the firm.

Regas informs Giles that she wants to temporarily put aside her personal relationship with him until the CAA audit is complete in two weeks. She suggests that, at the end of the two-week period, they get together and thoroughly examine the possible implications of their continued relationship. Giles reluctantly agrees, but he conditions his acceptance on having a "farewell" dinner at their favorite restaurant. Regas agrees to the dinner.

Giles and Regas have dinner that Saturday night. As luck would have it the controller of CAA Industries, Mark Sax, is at the restaurant with his wife. Sax is startled when he sees Giles and Regas together. He wonders about the possible seriousness of their relationship, while reflecting on the recent progress billings of the accounting firm. Sax believes that the number of hours billed is out of line with work of a similar nature billed on prior audits. Sax's first inclination is that the increased number of hours billed may be attributable to CAA's new accounting system. However, if the system was creating delays in completing the audit, Sax knows that he would have been informed about this by Barry Pasternak, the audit manager on the engagement. Sax and Pasternak met for two hours yesterday to discuss the status of the audit and when the firm would complete its fieldwork. Nothing was said about any problems auditing the system or its operations.

At this point Sax starts to wonder whether the reason for the high level of billings is sitting across from him in the restaurant. He decides that he will telephone Herb Morris, the managing partner of the office of the accounting firm and a friend of Sax, and further discuss this matter.

Sax and Morris meet on Monday to discuss Sax's concerns about seeing Giles and Regas at the restaurant and the possibility that their relationship is negatively affecting audit efficiency. Morris asks whether any other incidents have occurred to make him suspicious about the billings. Sax says that he is only aware of this one instance, although he sensed some apprehension on the part of Regas last week when they discussed why it was taking so long to get the audit recommendations for adjusting journal entries. Morris listens attentively until Sax finishes and then asks him to be patient while he sets up a meeting to discuss the situation with Giles. Morris promises to get back to Sax by the end of the week.

QUESTIONS

1. What is your assessment of the firm's policy on dating? What ethical concerns do you have about the relationship between Giles and Regas? Are Giles and Regas equally responsible for the tension it has created?

2. Given the facts of this case, what do you think Morris should say to Giles when they meet? In your response, consider how you would resolve the situation in regard to both the completion of the CAA Industries audit and the longer-term issue of the continued employment of Giles and Regas in the accounting firm. Be sure to evaluate these matters using ethical reasoning.

Jason Tybell

■

Jason Tybell has been employed as a junior accountant by the professional accountancy corporation of Rodgers & Philips for three years. Tybell graduated with a master of accountancy degree from a prestigious university outside Boston. He recently became a CPA and is looking forward to a long and successful career in the accounting profession.

Tybell is concerned about a meeting he will have later in the day with his mentor, William Jackson. Tybell has been worried lately about the fact that he was not asked to work on the current year's audit of two clients that he worked on during his first two years with the firm. Tybell knows that it is unusual to be taken off an audit unless a relationship develops that creates a conflict, such as when one's spouse or other close relative becomes involved with a client entity in a management decision-making function. He does not have this or any other conflict of interest with either of the two clients. Moreover, his performance evaluation reports on these two engagements were good. The seniors who filed the reports and reviewed them with Tybell seemed satisfied with his performance. In fact, no one in the firm has pointed out any problems with his performance on any engagements. He assumes that his mentor would counsel him about any such problems. Perhaps this is the purpose of the meeting.

At a recent meeting of the partners of Rodgers & Philips, Jackson was informed that a third client has complained about Tybell. As a result, Tybell is being removed from an audit for the third time. Upon investigation it was determined that in each situation the senior gave Tybell a good evaluation, but subsequently asked for his removal from future audits because of complaints about Tybell's inappropriate comments in meetings with client personnel. For example, in the current situation Tybell made a sarcastic comment at a meeting with the office manager. This was a meeting attended by the audit manager, the senior, another staff accountant, Tybell, and the client's office manager. The purpose of the meeting was to discuss the accounting firm's evaluation of client office procedures. The firm had very few suggestions for improvement, because the office now operates quite efficiently. The office manager, Michael Stevens, was hired one year ago and given the responsibility of restructuring the office and modernizing the procedures for information flow and internal controls. The office workers were largely unorganized and unsupervised prior to Stevens's arrival. He turned things around very quickly. The comment by Tybell that upset Stevens was in response to two statements. Stevens stated that he (Stevens) worked hard to get the office to run smoothly. The senior on the engagement then noted that Stevens spends more time in the office than did any of his predecessors. Tybell commented on these statements by saying: "That's not saying very much."

During the partners' meeting, Jackson asks whether anyone has ever spoken with Tybell about his tendency to make inappropriate comments around client personnel. No one could find a performance evaluation report that documented any such problem. It seems that Tybell has been evaluated as a competent accountant and one who always gets his work done on time. All of the seniors who have worked with him have been favorably impressed by his technical abilities. His ratings on communication skills are not quite as good, although his evaluations indicate no specific problems.

At this point in the meeting, Jackson suggests that he speak with Tybell about the latter's lack of tact in dealing with clients. However, the other partners do not feel that this is sufficient. As far as they are concerned, the "handwriting is on the wall." They do not believe that Tybell is partner material. One partner comments: "Tybell needs to be informed that his future at Rodgers & Philips is limited." Another partner agrees and expresses the general sentiment of all the partners, as follows:

> We can probably keep him here for one or two more years, but no longer than that. He will be eligible to be promoted to senior after four years. We can't take a chance on his making similar mistakes when he starts to supervise others. It may have a negative influence on staff accountants, and it presents a continuing problem regarding client contact. As we all know, the firm must be able to have confidence in all its staff and must feel certain that they have the necessary interpersonal skills to get along with clients.

At the meeting between William Jackson and Jason Tybell, Jackson informs Tybell that the firm can keep him on for one more year, but not longer than that. As Jackson describes the partners' concerns, he notices that Tybell does not seem a bit surprised. In fact, Tybell's reaction is to ask, "What took you so long?"

QUESTIONS

1. Evaluate the accounting firm's actions (or inactions) from an ethical reasoning perspective. In particular, what do you think about the performance evaluation system and Jason Tybell's treatment by Jackson and by the partners of the firm?

2. What do you think Jason Tybell might have meant by his final comment, "What took you so long?" If you were Tybell, what would be your reaction to Jackson after he had informed you of the basis for the decision regarding your future employment with the firm?

CASES

EXTERNAL REPORTING

Imperial Valley Thrift & Loan

■

Bill Stanley, of Jacobs, Stanley & Co., started to review the work-paper files on his client, Imperial Valley Thrift & Loan, in preparation for the audit of the client's financial statements for the year ended December 31, 1994. These preaudit statements submitted by the client are presented in Exhibit 1 on page 60.

Bill Stanley knew there were going to be some problems to contend with during the course of the audit, so he decided to review several items in the file in order to refresh his memory about the client's operations.

BACKGROUND

The first item Stanley reviewed was the planning memo he prepared about two months ago. This memo is summarized in Exhibit 2 on page 62.

The next item Stanley reviewed was an internal office communication on potential audit risks. This communication described three areas of particular concern.

1. The client charged off $420,000 in loans in 1993 and had already charged off $535,000 through July 31, 1994. Reserve requirements by law are a minimum of 1.25% of loans outstanding. However, given prior history, this statutory amount probably would not be large enough. This, in combination with the prior auditors' concerns about proper loan underwriting procedures and documentation, indicates that we should carefully review loan quality.

2. The audit report issued on the 1993 financial statements contained an explanatory paragraph describing the uncertainty about the client's ability to continue as a going concern. The concern was caused by the "capital impairment" declaration by the Department of Corporations.

EXHIBIT 1
Imperial Valley Thrift & Loan
Balance Sheet (preaudit)
December 31, 1994

Assets

Cash and cash equivalents	$1,960,000
Loans receivable	6,300,000
Less: Reserve for loan losses	(25,000)
Unearned discounts & fees	(395,000)
Accrued interest receivable	105,000
Prepayments	12,000
Real property held for sale	514,000
Property, plant, & equipment	390,000
Less: Accumulated depreciation	(110,000)
Contribution to Thrift Guaranty Corp.	15,000
Deferred start-up costs	44,000
Total assets	$8,810,000

Liabilities & Equity
Liabilities

Regular & money market savings	$2,212,000
T-bills & CDs	5,180,000
Accrued interest payable	190,000
Accounts payable & accruals	28,000
Total liabilities	$7,610,000

Equity

Capital stock	$ 700,000
Additional paid-in capital	1,120,000
Retained earnings (deficit)	(620,000)
Total equity	$1,200,000
Total liabilities and equity	$8,810,000

(continued)

3. The client had weak internal controls according to the prior auditors. Some of the items to look out for, in addition to proper loan documentation, were whether the preaudit financial statement information provided by the client is supported by the general ledger, whether the accruals were appropriate, and whether all transactions were properly authorized and recorded on a timely basis.

Audit Findings

The audit was conducted during January and February 1995. Based on information gathered during the audit, the following were the areas of greatest concern to Stanley:

EXHIBIT 1
Imperial Valley Thrift & Loan
Statement of Operations (preaudit)
For the Year Ended December 31, 1994

Revenues

Interest earned	$ 820,000
Discount earned	210,000
Investment income	82,000
Fees, charges, & commissions	78,000
Total revenues	$1,190,000

Expenses

Interest expense	$ 815,000
Provision for loan losses	180,000
Salary expense	205,000
Occupancy expense including depreciation	100,000
Other administrative expense	160,000
Legal expense	12,000
Thrift Guaranty Corp. payment	48,000
Total expenses	$1,520,000
Net loss for the year	$ 330,000

1. Adequacy of Loan Collateral.   A review of 30 loan files representing $2,100,000 of total loans outstanding (33.3% of the portfolio) indicated that much of the collateral for the loans was in the form of second or third mortgages on real property. This gave the client a potentially unenforceable position due to the existence of very large senior liens. For example, in the event foreclosure became necessary to collect Imperial Valley's loan, the client would have to first pay off these large senior liens. Other collateral often consisted of personal items such as jewelry and furniture. In the case of jewelry, often there was no effort made by the client after granting the loan to ascertain whether the collateral was still in the possession of the borrower. The jewelry could have been sold without the client's knowledge.

2. Collectibility of Loans.   Many loans were structured in such a way as to require interest payments only for a small number of years (two or three years), with a balloon payment for principal due at the end of this time. This structure made it difficult to properly evaluate the payment history of the borrower. Although the annual interest payments may have been made for the first year or two, this was not necessarily a good indication that the borrower would be able to pay off the principal on the loan. Additionally, there was no information in the financial statements that would indicate how the borrower would come up with the cash needed to make the large final payment.

EXHIBIT 2
Planning Memo

---

1. The firm of Jacobs, Stanley & Co. succeeded the firm of Nelson, Thomas & Co. as auditors for Imperial Valley Thrift & Loan. The prior auditors conducted the 1992 and 1993 audits. Jacobs, Stanley & Co. communicated in writing with Nelson, Thomas & Co. prior to acceptance of the engagement. Additionally, authorization was given by the client for a review of the predecessor auditors' working papers. The findings of these inquiries are summarized in item 6 below and the previously discussed internal office communication.

2. Imperial Valley Thrift & Loan was incorporated in California on June 12, 1988. It is a wholly owned subsidiary of Nuevo Financial Group, S.A., a Mexican corporation. As an industrial loan company, it is restricted to certain types of business, including making real estate and consumer loans and certain types of commercial loans.

3. Imperial Valley accepts deposits in the form of interest-bearing passbook accounts and investment certificates. Most of the depositors are of Spanish descent. The client primarily services the Spanish-speaking community in the Imperial Valley of southern California, which is a rural community located on the Mexican border.

4. The principal officers of Imperial Valley are Jose Ortega and his brother Arturo. They serve as the chief executive officer and the chief financial officer, respectively.

5. Imperial Valley is subject to the regulations of the California Industrial Loan Law and is examined by the Department of Corporations. It was last examined in December 1993 and was put on notice as "capital impaired." Additional capital was being sought from local investors.

6. Based on review of the prior auditors' working papers, the following items were noted:
   a. The client's lack of profitability was due to a high volume of loan losses resulting from poor underwriting procedures and faulty documentation.
   b. Imperial Valley has a narrow net interest margin due to the fact that all deposits are interest bearing and it pays the highest interest rates in the area.
   c. Due to the small size of the client and its focus on handling day-to-day operating problems, the internal controls are marginal at best. There were material weaknesses in their loan underwriting procedures and documentation, as well as in compliance with regulatory requirements.

---

3. Weaknesses in Internal Controls. Internal-control weaknesses were a pervasive concern. The auditors recomputed certain accruals and unearned discounts, confirmed loan and deposit balances, and reconciled the preaudit financial information provided by the client to the general ledger. Some adjustments had to be made as a result of this work. A material weakness in the lending function was identified. Loans were too frequently granted merely because the borrowers were well known to Imperial Valley officials, who believed they could be counted on to repay their outstanding loans. An ability to repay these loans was based too often on "faith," rather than on clear indications that the borrowers would have the necessary cash available to repay their loans when they came due. This was of great concern to the auditors, especially in light of the inadequacy of the loan reserve, as detailed in item 5, below.

4. Status of Additional Capital Infusion.   According to regulatory requirements, a thrift and loan institution must maintain a 6:1 ratio of thrift certificates to net equity capital. Based on the financial information provided by Imperial Valley, the capital deficiency was only $32,000 below capital requirements (preaudit), as follows:

Thrift certificates ratio	$\dfrac{\$7,392,000}{6}$
Net equity capital required	$1,232,000
Net equity capital reported	$1,200,000
Deficiency	$ 32,000

However, audit adjustments explained in Exhibit 3, on page 64, increased the capital deficiency to $622,000, as follows:

Net equity capital required	$1,232,000
Net equity capital (postaudit)	$ 610,000
Deficiency	$ 622,000

There was a possibility that the parent company, Nuevo Financial Group, would contribute the additional equity capital. Also, management had been in contact with a potential outside investor about the possibility of investing $600,000. This investor, Manny Gonzalez, had strong ties to the family ownership of Imperial Valley.

5. Adequacy of General Reserve Requirement.   The general reserve requirement of 1.25% had not been met. Based on the client's reported outstanding loan balance of $6,300,000, a reserve of $78,750 would be necessary. However, audit adjustments for the charge-off of uncollectible loan amounts significantly affected the amount actually required. Additionally, the auditors felt that a larger percentage would be necessary because of the client's history of problems with loan collections. Initially, a 5% rate was proposed. Management felt this was much too high, arguing that the company had improved its lending procedures in the last few months and that it expected to have a smaller percentage of charge-offs in the future. A current delinquent report received in February 1995 showed only two loans from 1994 still on the past-due list. The auditors agreed to a 2% reserve, and an adjusting entry (AJE #3) was made.

Exhibit 3, on page 64, presents the audit-adjusting entries affecting the loans receivable account and related reserve balance. Following AJE #3 is an explanation of this entry, excerpted from the working papers.

EXHIBIT 3
Audit Adjustments

AJE #1—Reserve for loan losses $200,000
            Loans receivable $200,000
     To write down loans to net
     realizable value
AJE #2—Reserve for loan losses 300,000
     Unearned discounts & fees 80,000
            Loans receivable 380,000
     To write off loans more than
     180 days past due in compliance
     with statutes
AJE #3—Provision for loan losses 590,000
            Reserve for loan losses 590,000
     To increase the reserve balance
     to 2% of outstanding loans
     as follows:
     Reserve balance (preaudit) . . . . $(25,000)
Less: Adjusting entry
  #1 . . . . $200,000
  #2 . . . . <u>300,000</u>
                                                <u>500,000</u>
  Subtotal $475,000
Add: Desired balance
Loan balance (preaudit) $6,300,000
Less: AJE #1 . . . . (200,000)
     #2 . . . . <u>(380,000)</u>
Loan balance (postaudit) $5,720,000
Reserve requirement 2%
Desired balance (approx.) . . . . <u>115,000</u>
  Adjustment required $590,000

REGULATORY ENVIRONMENT

Imperial Valley Thrift & Loan was approaching certain regulatory filing deadlines during the course of the audit. Stanley had a meeting with the regulators. Representatives of management were present at this meeting. Gonzalez also attended the meeting, since he had expressed some interest in possibly making a capital contribution. There was a lot of discussion about the ability of Imperial Valley to keep its doors open if the loan losses were recorded as proposed by the auditors. This was a concern because the proposed adjustments would place the client in a position of having net equity capital significantly below minimum requirements.

The regulators were concerned about the adequacy of the 2% general reserve because of the prior collection problems experienced by Imperial Valley. The institution's solvency was a primary concern. At the time of the meeting, the regulators were quite busy trying to straighten out problems caused by the failure of another thrift and loan in the state. Many depositors had lost money as a result of this failure. This created even greater concerns for the regulators regarding the position of Imperial Valley Thrift & Loan. Also, the regulators were unable to make a thorough audit of the company on their own, so they relied quite heavily on the work of Jacobs, Stanley & Co. In this sense the audit was used as leverage on the institution to get more money in as a cushion to protect depositors. The regulators viewed this as essential in light of the other thrift's failure and the fact that the insurance protection mechanism for thrift and loan depositors was less substantial than depository insurance available through FDIC for depositors in commercial banks and in savings and loan institutions.

SUMMARY OF CLIENT AND AUDITOR POSITIONS

The management of Imperial Valley Thrift & Loan placed a great deal of pressure on the auditors to reduce the amount of the loan write-offs. It maintained that the customers were "good for the money." Managers pointed out that payments to date on most of the loans had been made on a timely basis. However, it was the auditors' contention that the timeliness of payments to date, which were mostly annual interest amounts, was not necessarily a good indication that timely balloon principal payments would be made. They felt it was very difficult to adequately evaluate collectibility of the balloon payments, primarily because the borrowers' source of cash for loan repayment had not been identified. They could not objectively audit or support borrowers' good intentions to pay and undocumented resources as represented by client management.

The client felt that the auditors did not fully understand the nature of its business. Managers pointed out that a certain amount of risk had to be accepted in their business because they primarily made loans that commercial banks and savings and loan institutions did not want to make. The client managers felt that the auditors' inability to understand and appreciate this element of their business was the main reason the latter were having trouble evaluating collectibility on the outstanding loans.

In order to ensure that they were not being naive about the thrift and loan industry, the auditors checked with colleagues in another office of the firm who knew more about this type of business. One professional in this office explained that the real secret to this business is to follow up ruthlessly with nonpayers. The auditors certainly did not feel this was being done by the management of Imperial Valley.

The auditors knew that Manny Gonzalez was a potential source of investment capital for Imperial Valley. They felt it was very important to give Gonzalez an accurate picture, because if a rosier picture was painted than actually existed, and he were to make an investment, then the audit firm would be a potential target for a lawsuit.

AUDIT OPINION

The management of Imperial Valley Thrift & Loan was pressuring the auditors to give an unqualified opinion. If the auditors decided to give a qualified or an adverse opinion or to disclaim an opinion, then, in the client's view, this would present a picture to their customers and the regulators that their financial statements were not accurate. The client maintained this would be a blow to its integrity and would shake depositors' confidence in the institution.

On one hand, the auditors were very cognizant of their responsibility to the regulatory authority, and they were also concerned about providing an accurate picture of Imperial Valley's financial health to Manny Gonzalez or other potential investors. On the other hand, they wondered whether they were holding the client to standards that were too strict. After all, the audit report issued in the prior year by the previous auditors only contained an explanatory paragraph on the capital impairment issue. They also wondered whether the doors of the institution would be closed by the regulators if they gave an adverse opinion or disclaimed an opinion. What impact could this action have on the depositors? Bill Stanley wondered, whose interests are we really representing—depositors, shareholders, management, or regulators, or all of these?

Bill Stanley knew that he would soon have to make a recommendation about the type of audit opinion to be issued on the 1994 financial statements of Imperial Valley Thrift & Loan. Before approaching the advisory partner on the engagement, Stanley drafted the following memo to the file:

Memo: Going-Concern Question

The question of the going-concern status of Imperial Valley Thrift & Loan is being raised because of the client's continuing operating losses and high level of loan losses. The client lost $920,000 after audit adjustments in 1994. This is in addition to a loss of $780,000 in 1993. Imperial Valley has also reported a loss of $45,000 for the first two months of 1995.

Imperial Valley is also out of compliance with regulatory capital requirements. After audit adjustments, the client has net equity capital of $610,000 as of December 31, 1994. The Department of Corporations requires a 6:1 ratio of thrift certificates to capital. As of December 31, 1994, these regulations would require net equity capital of $1,232,000. Imperial Valley was therefore undercapitalized by $622,000 at that date, and no additional capital contributions have been made subsequent to December 31. It is possible, however, that either the parent company, Nuevo Financial Group, or a private investor, Manny Gonzalez, will contribute additional equity capital.

We have concluded that there is a substantial doubt as to the company's ability to continue in business. The reasons for this conclusion include the following:

- The magnitude of losses, particularly loan losses, indicates a possibility that Imperial Valley is not well managed.

- The losses are continuing in 1995. Annualized losses to date, without any provision for loan losses, are $270,000.
- Additional equity capital has not been contributed to date, although Gonzalez has $600,000 available.
- Our review of client loan files and lending policies raises an additional concern that loan losses may continue. If this happens, it would only exacerbate the conditions mentioned herein.

It would not be possible to test the liquidation value of the assets at this time should Imperial Valley not continue in business. The majority of client assets are loans receivable. These would presumably have to be discounted in order to be sold. In addition, there is some risk that the borrowers will simply stop making payments.

In conclusion, it is our opinion that a going-concern question exists for Imperial Valley Thrift & Loan at December 31, 1994. Pending the resolution of the question of capital adequacy, at a minimum, our audit report will include an explanatory paragraph describing the substantial doubt we have about Imperial Valley's ability to continue as a going concern.

QUESTIONS

Assume you are the advisory partner to Bill Stanley. It is your responsibility to review key memoranda and discussions with the client. Also, you are to counsel Stanley about the proper type of audit opinion to issue on the financial statements of Imperial Valley.

1. Identify the operational and accounting issues that should be considered by Stanley in evaluating how the issuance of the different types of audit opinions might affect those with competing interests?
2. What would be your advice to Stanley? Be sure to use the tools of ethical analysis in deciding on a course of action.

Software Innovations

∎

Tony Oliveri is a systems consultant for Edison and Franklin, a large regional public accounting firm located in the midwestern state of Chiana. Oliveri recently completed a job where he helped his client, the state of Chiana, prepare a request for proposals for computer hardware based on his firm's conceptual design of the applications software. The request for proposals carried with it a price tag of approximately $2 million for hardware to run the proposed software system. The client hired Edison and Franklin to either develop a custom package or identify software packages on the market that would satisfy the data processing needs of one of the agencies of the state government.

The state of Chiana had hired the accounting firm as systems consultants to help the agency develop or select applications software to do several things—investment analysis, cash management, debt management, and basic accounting functions. Oliveri felt that it would be best to first investigate software already available on the market because, if the firm could find a package that would meet the needs of the client, the firm could save a great deal of time and money for the client by not having to develop a custom package. Oliveri decided to do a software survey in the investment analysis area, which represented 30–40% of the total client need. In Oliveri's opinion, this was the most important need to fill.

Based on the software evaluation, Oliveri concluded that one software package, Congruence, would meet all the requirements of the client and was far superior to any other available package. Available through Software Innovations, it was an integrated package that utilized database management technology. It was not only an exceptional package for investment analysis but would also be quite effective for the other functions required by the client.

The client had insisted that the hardware proposed be capable of running the software package. The software package selected by Oliveri would run only on one of four major hardware vendors' systems, or a compatible system. Oliveri was concerned that the other three hardware vendors might protest the selection, because they were effectively excluded from the competition on the basis of the software selection. He knew this would always be a concern when operating in a state environment where the requirement exists to issue a request for proposals. Also, since the procurement was a very large one, this might provide an additional incentive for protest.

Although Oliveri was concerned about reaction to the software selection, he was convinced that, from a business point of view, the software selected was the best available package. He also felt good about the fact that his client had agreed with him. Still, he had an uneasy feeling about the selection. He decided to recapitulate the important factors he had considered, in addition to the primary one—that Congruence best fit the conceptual design and had all the functions and features his client wanted in a software package.

It was routine procedure to review a checklist of considerations in selecting a software package and a vendor. Some of these considerations included:

- Making a site visit to the vendor to see its operations
- Talking to clients of the vendor and assessing serviceability
- Evaluating the financial condition of the vendor
- Evaluating the stability of the vendor
- Evaluating the vendor's maintenance record
- Ascertaining whether the vendor had a help desk

During the investigation of Software Innovations, Oliveri discovered, through a casual conversation with a friend of his on the audit staff, that the company was an audit client of his firm. He also discovered that the firm issued an audit report with an unqualified opinion on the prior years' financial statements and that the report contained an explanatory paragraph describing the going-concern issue. The audit for the current year was not scheduled for another eight or nine months. Oliveri was concerned about this discovery—partly because of the way it came to light. Ordinarily, a request would be made by the Management Advisory Services (MAS) client for the annual financial statements of the vendor to assess the vendor's financial condition. In this case, the financial condition was discovered before any such request could be made. Since Software Innovations was not a publicly held company, the financial information was not publicly available. The company's financial condition and the existence of a going-concern issue were not discovered through independent inquiry—the usual manner of uncovering such knowledge in this kind of situation.

Oliveri told his client to request financial statement information from Software Innovations even though he knew what these statements would indicate. He wanted to make sure that his client was aware of the firm's uncertainty about the entity's ability to continue as a going concern. He wanted the client to discover this fact for itself.

Oliveri informed Software Innovations that the nature of the audit opinion was going to come to light and that he intended to discuss this with government officials from the state of Chiana after they had a chance to review the financial statement information. This was not of great concern to the company since, in its view, it could adequately explain and respond to any concerns about its status as a company. In fact, it had prepared a document that presented its viewpoint in reaction to the going-concern issue.

Oliveri had extensive discussions with his client about Software Innovations and whether the going-concern status of the entity should affect their decision to select the Congruence package. There was no doubt that the applications package was the best one available. Oliveri and the client were of the opinion that even if Software Innovations went out of business in a year or two, this fact would not significantly affect the decision, since the state of Chiana would still derive most of the benefit from using the package. Also, the client would probably have its own maintenance capability by that time. One potential negative factor was the lost capability of benefiting from any software enhancements if Software Innovations were to go out of business. Having carefully considered all factors, the client agreed with Oliveri that the Congruence package was so perfect for its needs that one requirement of the request for proposals should be that the hardware be capable of running this software package.

As a final step before issuing his recommendation, Oliveri had an audit advisory partner of the firm review the factors considered by the systems consultants in making their selection. He wanted to be sure the selection was sound and supportable. The partner agreed that there was a careful and thorough review of relevant factors and that a sound basis existed for the software selection.

Oliveri has now completed his review of the facts surrounding the selection of the applications package of Software Innovations. He is now focusing on the future. He is aware that protests can be filed on the request for proposals any time up until the contract award, which was still six months in the future. He is wondering whether there will be protests from some of the hardware vendors, since the selected software cannot run on their machines. If so, what form will these protests take? He is also quite concerned about "appearances," because of the facts of this case.

QUESTIONS

1. Do you think that Tony Oliveri and his firm have handled the situation in an ethical manner from a rights and justice point of view?
2. Using appropriate ethical analysis, discuss what you would do if you were in Oliveri's position and Software Innovations told you that it did not want to release its financial statements to your consulting client, the state of Chiana?

Bubba Tech, Inc. (BTI)

■

Willie Carson and Waylon Boone are friends who grew up in Dallas, Texas. They both attended the University of Texas at Austin and graduated with degrees in accounting and computer sciences, respectively. They moved back to Dallas after graduation. Carson went to work for the accounting firm of Randy Burnham & Co. This firm was one of the largest accounting firms in the world, and it was considered to be an expert in accounting for companies in the high-tech industry. Boone went to work for Alorotom, Inc., which was one of the largest manufacturers of high-tech products in the world.

Carson and Boone worked for these companies for seven years. During this time Carson became a certified public accountant, while Boone successfully completed a master's degree program in information systems at Southern Methodist University. In 1981 they decided to strike out on their own, and they formed a high-tech manufacturing company.

Carson and Boone decided to open their business in Austin, because the business community there was attempting to diversify into the high-tech area by providing incentives and support to attract companies operating in this sector. The business community felt that it could emulate the success of the high-tech industry in Dallas. This was considered to be very important to the continued economic growth and development in Austin.

Carson and Boone became the chief financial officer and the chief executive officer, respectively, of their new company, Bubba Tech, Inc. (BTI). Following two years of rapid business growth, and with excellent future prospects, BTI decided to "go public" in 1983. In conjunction with BTI's public sale of stock, the company contracted with Randy Burnham & Co. to audit its historical financial statements and assist in the filing of registration information with the SEC. The accounting firm was very helpful to BTI in this regard, as well as in assisting the company in setting up a data processing system.

Subsequent to a successful public stock offering, Randy Burnham & Co. continued to provide auditing services for BTI. The firm did not have an office in Austin. It serviced BTI from Dallas. It was not unusual for Randy Burnham to service clients from a larger office in another city when the firm only had one major client in a smaller city. In fact, only two large accounting firms had offices in Austin in 1983. Only one of these two firms, Tanner, Lidiak & Co., was an expert in the high-tech industry. That firm was a major competitor of Randy Burnham for clients in this industry.

The partner in charge of the BTI audit was Roger Metzger. From the beginning, there was an issue with the client over the size of the fee that the firm was charging. The CEO, Waylon Boone, told Metzger he was very concerned about this issue. The firm felt the fee was appropriate in light of the quality of service rendered and its need to cover costs incurred on the job.

The managing partner of Tanner, Lidiak & Co. developed close relationships with the leaders of the Austin business community. He had an opportunity to work with several members of the board of directors of BTI. By developing strong personal relationships, and by having a very visible local presence, the managing partner became very highly regarded by some members of the board of BTI. This fact, coupled with the element of competition for clients in the high-tech industry, created an environment in which Randy Burnham & Co. was concerned about potential competition from Tanner, Lidiak & Co. for the BTI audit.

During the years 1984–1991, BTI experienced great success, evidenced by a tripling of sales revenue and excellent future prospects. Randy Burnham continued to provide auditing services, as well as tax and some consulting services. In fact, BTI had become one of the larger clients for the Dallas office of the firm.

In 1991, Metzger decided it would be best to reconsider the amount of fees being charged to BTI. He was concerned about the potential for the fee issue to negatively affect the relationship of his firm with BTI. This seemed especially necessary in light of the continuing influence of Tanner, Lidiak & Co. in the Austin business community and with some members of the board of BTI. After careful review, Metzger told Waylon Boone that, although the firm did not think its base fee was out of line, it would restrict future fee increases to correspond with future increases in the cost of living.

At the first meeting of the audit committee in 1991, a new member of the board of directors and the audit committee, Gale Yarbord, whose family was very well established in the Austin business community, charged that the billing rates of Randy Burnham & Co. were much too high. Metzger knew there was a potential problem.

Over the next few years, the firm attempted to keep its fees within the established guidelines. It better utilized the work of the internal audit department of BTI. Metzger made every effort to keep management informed about the audit work of his firm. Each year through 1993, management approved the fee of Randy Burnham & Co., as did the audit committee and the board of directors. However, there was always a degree of tension about the fee charged.

In early 1994, Randy Burnham & Co. decided to open an office in Austin. Metzger hoped this would help his firm in its relationship with BTI. In October 1994, Metzger was to meet with the audit committee for the annual preaudit planning meeting. He had cleared the audit fee estimate in advance with management, as he had always done. Waylon Boone raised the issue of the size of the fee. However, he supported the estimate, especially in light of the quality of services provided by the accounting firm to BTI during the prior 11 years. Willie Carson had always been a strong supporter of the firm, not only because of its service to BTI but also based on its outstanding national reputation as an accounting firm in general and, specifically, in the high-tech industry.

During the meeting with the audit committee, Metzger was informed by the chair of the committee, J. L. Harley, that the committee had held a private meeting earlier in the week, at which time it decided to request proposals from other CPA firms. Harley informed Metzger that the issue was not the quality of services provided by Randy Burnham but a continuing concern about the size of the fee. The audit committee decided that, in order to demonstrate "due diligence," it had to go out and seek proposals.

After the meeting with the audit committee, Metzger met with Carson and Boone, who appeared to be just as surprised as Metzger, because they had approved the audit fee estimate. They claimed to have no advance knowledge of the audit committee's actions. They reiterated the concern of the board of directors about the fees charged. However, Metzger knew it was more complicated than this. He felt that management had not been properly involved in the audit committee's decision. Metzger recognized that BTI was unique in that its board of directors appeared to be much stronger relative to management than would be the case in most companies.

At this point, Metzger reflected on the composition of the audit committee. Seven of the eleven members of the board of directors also served on the audit committee. Three of these seven members had close ties with the firm Tanner, Lidiak & Co. This firm had done a good deal of accounting and tax work for business entities owned by these members. Two other members were very active in the Greater Austin Chamber of Commerce. They were also strong supporters of Tanner, Lidiak & Co., especially since the firm had helped to bring new business to Austin. The final two members of the committee were considered to be supporters of Randy Burnham & Co. Over the years, these members expressed satisfaction with the quality of services the firm performed for BTI.

In December 1994 the management of BTI tried to stop the board from seeking proposals from other audit firms. The managers were not successful. The board proceeded, stating that the time had come for it to demonstrate due diligence.

The firm of Randy Burnham & Co. went through the process of competitive bidding to retain the BTI audit, which it had been doing for 11 years. The firm always felt its fees were fair, yet it knew that the fees were at a higher level than the Austin business community was accustomed to paying for audit services. Roger

Metzger wondered: "How do you retain your credibility and professionalism and still be competitive?"

The firm was at full recovery based on its billing rates. It reduced its price to 80% of its normal fees, which was a big discount—although not unique in the current environment of competitive bidding. It did not want to lose BTI as a client, because the company was important to its high-tech practice in the southwestern United States. Also, the firm had just opened an office in Austin, hoping to expand its operations. It was the firm's position that if it lost BTI as a client, this would hurt its image with the local business community.

There were four firms bidding for the audit, in addition to Randy Burnham & Co. However, Metzger knew the firm's only real competition would come from Tanner, Lidiak & Co. In order to minimize the possibility of underbidding, Metzger suggested to Boone that he require a four-year contract with a fixed price for each year. If someone wanted the job, they would have to live with the proposal for four years. Metzger knew that a four-year commitment was a much longer one than most firms would want to make. A four-year fixed-fee proposal would also protect BTI from a sharp increase in fees if the firm selected had low-balled the first year's fee. Metzger felt that a four-year fixed-fee proposal would make the bidding process fairer to all concerned. Boone supported this position. He and Carson were successful in getting the board of directors to agree to the four-year fixed-fee requirement in seeking proposals.

In the debriefing, Metzger learned that his firm's bid was close to that of Tanner, Lidiak & Co. but not as low. The latter firm was selected as the new auditors. Metzger also learned that a management team from BTI had made its own separate evaluation of the proposals and had recommended to the audit committee that Randy Burnham & Co. be retained based on the need to balance service and fees. However, the committee decided to accept the bid of Tanner, Lidiak & Co. The final vote was 5-0, with two abstentions. The five members who voted to accept the bid of Tanner, Lidiak & Co. were those who had relationships with the firm through their own businesses or from their work with the Greater Austin Chamber of Commerce.

It is now three months after the decision by the board of directors to accept the bid of Tanner, Lidiak & Co. Metzger is sitting in his office thinking about one of the last things that Boone had said to him after the decision had been made. He had said: "From a fee standpoint, it was close enough so that an evaluation could have been made in favor of any firm based on a need to balance service and fees." This statement prompted Metzger to contemplate whether he would do anything differently if he had it all to do over again. He recalled that BTI spends about $300–$350 million each year. The audit fee was about $100,000–$125,000. This didn't seem very significant in relation to overall spending. Were the shareholders' interests fairly represented in the decision to change auditors? Metzger also contemplated the role of the audit committee of BTI in the decision to change auditors.

QUESTIONS

1. What do you think should be the proper relationship between an audit committee, the board of directors, management, and the external auditors? What factors affected this type of relationship in the BTI case? What actions might have been taken by Randy Burnham & Co. to mitigate the effect of these factors?

2. What is meant by the "due diligence position" of the audit committee? Were the interests of all stakeholders fairly represented in the decision to change auditors?

Linex Corporation

■

Linex was incorporated in Georgia in 1990 by two computer programmers, Bob Jason and John Hall. The company developed software for personal computers, with an emphasis on applications for the growing market of desktop publishing. Jason became the chief executive officer because of his administrative experience, while Hall was in charge of new product development.

Linex contracted with an Atlanta, Georgia, CPA firm, Simpson, Lafferty & Co., to audit its financial statements. The CPA firm issued audit reports with unqualified opinions for each of the years 1990–1994. In 1993 Linex went public, in part to help finance development of new software for the desktop publishing industry. This product, Prep-aid, enabled users to type presentation material in outline form and have it automatically formatted into transparencies. The product was targeted for business professionals and educators, who frequently used transparencies when making presentations.

Linex was very successful in 1995, in part due to strong sales of Prep-aid. It had now become one of the largest software companies specializing in desktop publishing. The company expected to expand its operations nationally during 1996. One event that occurred during December 1995, however, created a potential problem for Linex. Linex was named as a defendant in a patent infringement suit by a competitor, Datacore, Inc. Datacore alleged in the lawsuit that Linex infringed on its patent rights in relation to one of its software products that was very similar to Prep-aid.

In March 1996, Peter Thomas, partner in charge of the Linex audit, was completing the audit report on the December 31, 1995, financial statements. He contacted the attorney for Linex in order to determine the expected outcome of the lawsuit. Only preliminary hearings and discovery proceedings were in progress at this time. The attorney stated, however, that similar patent cases typically had been resolved in favor of the defendant. Therefore, the attorney was of the opinion that although it was possible that the decision would go against Linex, there was a less-than-50% likelihood of losing.

A meeting was held between Thomas and Jason to discuss the financial statement disclosure of the litigation uncertainty. Thomas indicated the accounting firm's position was that the litigation uncertainty should be explained in the financial statements, because the $5 million amount of the lawsuit was material. Jason stated he could not support this position, indicating that he was very concerned about the potential effect of such disclosure on Linex's ability to finance its operations as they expanded nationally. Thomas did express sensitivity to this position. He told Jason, however, that the firm had made a professional judgment that it was proper to disclose the event. Jason reiterated his dissatisfaction with this position, stating that Linex might have to seek proposals from other CPA firms for the audit of the December 31, 1996, financial statements.

Very little progress had been made in resolving the patent infringement lawsuit during the first nine months of 1996. In September 1996, Jason contacted Thomas, with a request for the submission of a proposal for the audit of the December 31, 1996, financial statements. Shortly thereafter, and unbeknownst to Thomas, Jason contacted two additional CPA firms, inviting them to submit proposals as well.

The primary reason for Jason's seeking proposals from other CPA firms was his unhappiness with the disclosure in the prior year's financial statements. He was also concerned about the potential position of Simpson, Lafferty & Co. on the litigation issue in the current year's statements.

One of the two CPA firms contacted was Donaldson, Holmes & Irwin. This firm was quite anxious to have Linex Corporation as a client because of the latter's successes in developing software applications for the expanding desktop publishing market. Additionally, the firm was aware that Linex would be seeking general management consulting services next year. It hoped to be able to provide these potentially lucrative services for the company.

All three CPA firms submitted proposals for the audit of Linex Corporation. Ultimately, the company accepted the proposal of Donaldson, Holmes & Irwin. This firm's bid was about 15% below the bids of the other two firms. Donaldson's bid was, however, contingent on also obtaining the consulting work. Linex's acceptance of this bid committed it to engaging Donaldson to do the consulting work.

QUESTIONS

1. In this case, Peter Thomas indicated it was the position of Simpson, Lafferty & Co. that the $5 million amount of the lawsuit was material. What factors should be considered by an auditor in judging the materiality of an uncertainty such as a lawsuit in reference to the need for financial statement disclosures?

2. What ethical questions can be raised by the facts of this case with respect to Linex's decision to seek proposals and to accept the bid of Donaldson, Holmes & Irwin?

Edvid, Inc.

■

Charles Hutton is the partner in charge of the Edvid, Inc., audit for the Big Six accounting firm of Pedcap & Twylan LLP. The firm was hired in February 1995 to replace a local firm that had serviced Edvid for the past five years. Edvid believes that it will be more successful with its pending stock offering in January 1996 if a Big Six firm audits the October 31, 1995, fiscal year-end financial statements.

Hutton was sitting in his office, preparing for a meeting with the practice director of his accounting firm. The purpose of the meeting was to discuss options available to the firm in light of one of its clients' ultimatums that the firm either agree to the client's accounting for profit on rental contracts the way the client proposes or the client would seek proposals from other independent public accounting firms in order to find a firm that agrees with the proposed accounting.

BACKGROUND

Edvid prepares educational and professional development videotapes for sale and rental to customers. It was acquired in a series of transactions by, and became a wholly owned subsidiary of, Software Technology Corp. (STC) on September 11, 1993. STC acquired Edvid to add educational and professional development videotape production and distribution to its very successful line of professional computer software packages.

Edvid's marketing approach was to develop a videotape library available to customers wishing to rent tapes. Customers would sign a subscription contract for a substantial initial payment, with monthly payments to be made over a two-year contract period. The contract entitled them to rent two tapes per month, drawing from approximately 1,500 educational and professional development training courses. Selections were mailed to them each month, and they had to return them to the videotape library within a certain time. Additional tapes could be rented for additional fees. Once tapes were rented, mailed out, and received, customers could not return any of the tapes for credit unless they received a defective tape or the wrong tape. This happened from time to time but was not considered a significant problem for Edvid. Edvid regularly acquired and/or produced tapes for its library, capitalizing the cost of such tapes for financial reporting purposes. Exhibit 1 reflects the terms of a sample rental contract.

ACCOUNTING FOR PROFIT BY EDVID

In the financial statements for the fiscal year ended October 31, 1994, Edvid followed the practice of accounting for rental contracts under the *modified operating method*. Under this method, revenue is recorded as the assets are used or the min-

EXHIBIT 1
Edvid, Inc.
Terms of Rental Contract

Total contract price		$700
Contract life		2 years
Payment terms		
Initial payment	$280	
Quarterly billings		
(7 quarters at $60.00 ea.)	420	
		$700

The contract holder has the right to borrow two tapes per month from the library. Additional tapes may be borrowed at $15.00 each.

Direct costs associated with contract:		
Royalties—incurred as tapes are used		
by customers	$100	
Servicing—incurred as tapes are used		
by customers	120	
		$220
Initial direct costs:*		
Advertising and promotion	$ 40	
Sales salaries	45	
Telephone, postage, and printing of marketing		
department	15	
Marketing studies	30	
		130
Total direct cost		$350

*These are incremental costs incurred to obtain and successfully complete the contracts. Under SFAS No. 91, "Accounting for Nonrefundable Fees and Costs Associated with Originating or Acquiring Loans and Initial Direct Costs of Leases," these costs should be amortized against earnings equally over the two-year contract period. Note that indirect costs—such as administrative expense, depreciation of tapes, and rent—are excluded in this analysis, as they should be expensed as period costs.

Other assumptions: (1) Interest factor is excluded. (2) Tape usage (and therefore royalty and servicing costs) are even over the two years.

imum fee is billed (if such billing approximates usage), and the related expenses are recorded to match revenues. Contribution margin recognition under this approach approximates straight-line recognition. Exhibit 2 reflects profit (contribution margin) recognition under this approach.

EXHIBIT 2
Edvid, Inc.
Profit Recognition—
Modified Operating Method

Year	Average Revenue	Initial Direct Costs	Royalties	Service Costs	Total Costs	Contrib. Margin
1	$350*	$ 65	$ 50	$ 60	$175	$175
2	350	65	50	60	175	175
Total	$700	$130	$100	$120	$350	$350

*Average revenue per year = $700/2 = $350

On April 22, 1995, subsequent to the issuance of the January 31, 1995, unaudited financial statements, the chief financial officer of STC requested an opinion with respect to accounting for rental contracts subsequent to October 1994. The CFO pointed out that 50% of the profit contribution (total contract revenue less initial direct costs, royalties and servicing costs, all discounted at appropriate interest rates) is now recognized at the date the contract is signed and that the remaining 50% should be recognized straight-line over the life of the contract. Exhibit 3 reflects profit recognition under the new method.

The CFO attempted to justify the accounting change by emphasizing that the rental contracts really represented a sale-and-purchase agreement with customers

EXHIBIT 3
Edvid, Inc.
Profit Recognition—
New Method

Year	Revenue Recognized	Initial Direct Costs	Royalties	Service Costs	Total Costs	Contrib. Margin*
1	$434†	$ 65	$ 50	$ 60	$175	$259
2	266	65	50	60	175	91
Total	$700	$130	$100	$120	$350	$350

*50% × $350 = $175   recognized at contract execution
11/23 × $175 =   84   recognized during first year (rounded to $)
      $259   total recognized during first year
12/23 × $175 =   91   recognized during second year (rounded to $)
      $350
†First-year contribution + first-year costs = $259 + $175 = $434 as first-year revenue recognition.

for the *right* to withdraw videotapes from the library. According to the CFO, "the biggest part of our costs is related to the marketing effort, which is complete when the contract is signed, and not the contract servicing. Therefore, we should not be treating the initial subscription fee as unearned revenue, as was done under the modified operating method, but we should recognize this fee as revenue immediately."

The CFO also pointed to two Statements of Financial Accounting Standards which, in his opinion, supported the new method. Summary excerpts from the first of these statements follows:

SFAS No. 48, "Revenue Recognition When Right of Return Exists" (Paragraph 6)

Under this statement, revenue recognition is appropriate when the right of return exists if all the following conditions are met:

1. The seller's price to the buyer is substantially fixed or determinable at the date of sale.
2. The buyer has paid the seller, or the buyer is obligated to pay the seller, and the obligation is not contingent on resale of the product.
3. The buyer's obligation to the seller would not be changed in the event of theft or physical destruction or damage of the product.
4. The buyer acquiring the product for resale has economic substance apart from that provided by the seller.
5. The seller does not have significant obligations for future performance to directly bring about the resale of the product by the buyer.
6. The amount of future returns can be reasonably estimated.

The CFO felt that the rental contract "sale" of rights qualified for immediate revenue recognition at the time of sale, since all of these conditions have been met.

The CFO felt that, although the second statement (summarized below) applied directly to motion picture and television activities, it could also be applied to producers and distributors of videotapes. The CFO interpreted the requirements of this statement as follows (interpretations in parentheses).

SFAS No. 53, "Financial Reporting by Producers and Distributors of Motion Picture Films" (Paragraph 6)

A licensor (lessor) shall recognize revenue for a license (rental) agreement for television program material when the license (rental) period begins *and* all of the following conditions have been met:

1. The license (rental) fee for each film (videotape) is known.
2. The cost of each film (videotape) is known or reasonably determinable.
3. Collectibility of the full license (rental) fee is reasonably assured.
4. The film (videotape) has been accepted by the licensee (lessee) in accordance with the conditions of the license (rental) agreement.

5. The film (videotape) is available for its first showing or telecast (viewing).

In addition to meeting these conditions, the CFO pointed out that, under SFAS No. 53, licensors (lessors) are supposed to consider a license (rental) agreement for television program (videotape) material as a sale of a right or a group of rights.

The CFO insisted that all the conditions for immediate revenue recognition under these two statements were met and, therefore, the company's new accounting method should be acceptable. The company strongly felt that its contract agreements represented the sale of a right with a nominal service component. Under its new approach, earnings are recognized on the product sale portion, and substantial revenues (equivalent to one-half the direct contribution margin) are deferred in order to provide a contribution margin at the time of future service. The client felt its method better reflects the following facts, which are consistent with the requirements of the two accounting statements previously mentioned:

- The principal portion of the transaction involves the client's right to the product.
- Payments are fixed under a noncancelable agreement.
- The fee must be paid by the client, regardless of usage.
- The costs are reasonably estimable.
- Future returns from customers, owing to the receipt of defective tapes or tapes not ordered, can be reasonably estimated.
- The company has only nominal future service obligations.

The CFO pointed to the following two additional considerations in adopting the new accounting method:

- Prior to November 1, 1994, agreements were written by Edvid with substantially different terms and conditions. In those circumstances, a revenue-recognition approach based on usage was appropriate. Revenues and income on these agreements will continue to be recorded by the company based on this approach. However, the new method will be used for the current contracts, since the company believes this method better reflects revenue earned on these contracts.
- Consolidated earnings for the three months ended January 31, 1995, would have been approximately $600,000 less if the company continued to use the modified operating method for rental contracts entered into in fiscal 1995. This would have a significant effect on the overall profitability of STC.

ACCOUNTANTS' VIEW

Charles Hutton informed the CFO of Edvid that the new accounting for rental contracts is not consistent with the intended effect of the revenue-recognition rules. The accounting firm's position is explained in the following paragraphs.

As regards the applicability of SFAS No. 48, the firm did not believe this statement applied to Edvid's situation. Hutton pointed out that the conditions for immediate revenue recognition pertain to situations where there is a sale of a product—not of a right. The type of situation envisioned under this statement is where there is a sale of a product and the buyer has the right of return during a trial examination period. These facts do not fit the rental contract characteristics of Edvid.

The accounting firm's position also was that SFAS No. 53 did not apply to Edvid, for the following reasons:

1. This statement is specifically intended for companies in the entertainment industry. Edvid is not in this industry. Further, the part of the statement that permits recognition of revenue at the date a contract is signed is intended only for a unique part of the entertainment industry—television exhibition. Edvid describes itself as part of a "professional services organization" involved in "producing and distributing video-assisted training courses." This does not qualify Edvid as being involved in "television exhibition."

2. SFAS No. 53 contemplates that future service must be minimal if profit is to be recognized at the date a contract is signed. Even if Edvid qualified for coverage under this statement, the future service would not be minimal, for the following reasons:

   a. Edvid provides for notification to customers of changes to be made to the present library sources.

   b. The company agrees to make available specialists to consult with its customers who may be having a problem with training courses.

   c. Future conferences, seminars, and newsletters are provided to customers free of charge. Therefore, they have future service implications.

   d. The company expressly or implicitly agrees to update the library.

Hutton also informed the CFO that it is only proper to recognize revenue (under the realization concept) when two conditions have been met:

1. The earnings process is complete or virtually complete.
2. Revenue is evidenced by the existence of an exchange transaction that has taken place.

The firm's position is that neither condition had been met. Since future service was a significant factor, the earnings process was not virtually complete. Also, an exchange transaction had not taken place until the customer requested tapes from the library.

Charles Hutton concluded by restating his firm's position that the company should have continued to use the modified operating method in the January 31, 1995, quarterly statements. Additionally, the company should use this method for all subsequent reporting periods. The CFO rejected this and insisted that the new method is in accordance with accounting rules. The CFO made it clear that the company intended to use this method—whether or not it had the support of the accounting firm.

QUESTIONS

1. Follow the seven-step ethical decision-making process and reason out what the accounting firm should do in this situation.

2. Assume that Edvid decided to switch back to the modified operating method subsequent to the issuance of the January 31, 1995, quarterly financial statements because of the accounting firm's threat to resign and report the difference of opinion to the SEC. How should this decision affect the quarterly statements for the remainder of fiscal 1995 and the October 31, 1995, year-end statements?

Engineering Associates

■

"Great news, Bill! I just found out that our proposal was accepted by Engineering Associates. Apparently, the company selected us because we are very familiar with the particular software the company wants to use and because it needs our business expertise in designing and installing the software for its new financial management system. We should have a meeting with our team to discuss our responsibilities and the relationship we will have with Engineering Associates."

Elliot Wolf is a consulting partner in the firm of Oken, Edelman, and Kramer. He has just informed Bill Nelson, senior consulting manager, that their firm has been selected for the $2 million job to install a financial management system for Engineering Associates. The client is an engineering consulting firm that has experienced a great deal of growth in its business during the past few years. At the present time, the engineering firm is manually processing its financial transactions. The accounting firm was hired to assist in the design and installation of the following:

1. **Accounts Payable and General Ledger.** The automation of accounts payable and general ledger functions was to be accomplished by adapting standard software packages to the needs of the client.

2. **Payroll System.** The payroll function was to be accomplished through the use of a bank payroll service.

3. **Billing System.** The billing system design was custom work. The firm was to work with Engineering Associates to identify the characteristics of their billings and to design a system that could be used to process billings to their clients.

Elliot Wolf and Bill Nelson met later in the week to discuss their responsibilities in the design and installation of the financial management system for Engineering Associates. They were concerned about the requirement of their client that one of its engineers, Perry Marks, serve as the project manager on the job. Marks had been successful in this position on some of the organization's past engineering projects. Therefore, the management of Engineering Associates felt that he could also manage the design and installation of the new computer system.

Wolf and Nelson were concerned because, typically, their firm would co-manage this type of project. It was the accounting firm's position that joint responsibility worked best. In this way, the firm would be able to bring issues to management as they arose. It would also have partial responsibility for resolving problems as they developed. There would always be some problems to contend with in the design and installation of a new computer system. Wolf and Nelson wondered how these problems would be resolved, since Marks was to serve as the sole project manager.

Marks was a young engineer with a master's degree who had joined Engineering Associates less than three years ago. Wolf and Nelson were not sure Marks had the necessary business expertise to effectively deal with the responsibility of being sole project manager. Also, there was no past history of working with the engineering firm to jointly resolve any issues or problems that might develop in the course of an engagement. Under these circumstances, Wolf and Nelson were particularly concerned about not having joint responsibility for project management. This factor caused them to view the engagement as risky. However, they were willing to accept this risk because the engagement represented a significant job, and there was a possibility of getting additional work from Engineering Associates if the computer system was successfully installed and if it operated the way everyone hoped that it would.

The accounting firm assigned one of its junior consulting managers to oversee the day-to-day operations of the firm's staff assigned to the job. Since the firm was concerned about the risks inherent in its relationship with the client, it was decided that Nelson should devote one day each week to reviewing progress on the job, even though this was not part of the accounting firm's contract for services.

Nelson knew that a great deal of emphasis was placed on meeting deadlines for installation of various phases of the system. This was largely because it had become very difficult for the client to keep up with its data processing needs through the use of its manual system.

At the beginning, Nelson thought everything was going according to schedule. However, it became clear over time that certain key steps were not being completed in an acceptable manner. Specifically, certain stages of the early design phase had not been carried out correctly. Perry Marks did not always obtain the necessary user sign-offs. He would allow the implementation to proceed from one phase to the next, without ensuring that all of the functions of the system in a particular phase were complete and documented. It was not always clear how the software would accommodate all of the necessary functions of the system. In short, Nelson discovered that there were many inaccuracies and that design documentation was often incomplete. These problems were identified in the accountants' status reports, which were given to the project manager, Perry Marks.

Bill Nelson's primary concern was that once a particular phase of the job was assumed to be completed, the staff had to move on to the next phase. However, each phase was dependent on the prior phase. If there were inaccuracies and incompleteness in one phase, they would affect the successful completion of later phases of the project.

Nelson knew that Marks was part of the problem. He was inexperienced in business management and, because of pressure to complete various phases of the project within the time projections, he was only concerned with meeting deadlines. In addition, he was not spending enough of his time supervising the project. Marks was supposed to devote 70 to 80% of his time to the project. However, he only devoted about one day each week to managing the project. In Nelson's opinion, Marks was not doing what was necessary in order to assure the installation of a quality financial management system.

As an example of this, after a given phase of the job was completed, Marks's staff would hand him a binder of documents describing the steps taken to complete the particular phase. He would accept the information at face value. As far as he was concerned, a phase was completed once he received the report from his staff. Nelson knew, however, that the staff's work did not always meet the quality level necessary to constitute true completion of a particular phase. He tried on several occasions to point this out to Marks. However, Marks's reaction typically was to say something like, "I'm taking responsibility for the status reports to management as the project manager. We hired you as our contractors. Don't worry about it. Just keep your nose to the grindstone and get things done by the deadline dates."

Bill Nelson had a very difficult time accepting this kind of attitude. He felt that, as a professional systems consultant, he should be sharing responsibility for the job and, certainly, he should have a client who was willing to listen to his suggestions and concerns. It was his impression that Marks felt that he was causing conflict rather than trying to avoid it. Nelson was afraid that the incipient problems he was identifying would come to light as the project progressed, and it would then be too late to correct them without spending a substantial amount of additional time and money.

The biggest area of concern for Bill Nelson was the job cost billing system. While the other elements of the financial system entailed adapting standard packages to the client's needs, the billing system had to be custom-designed. The staff of Engineering Associates had identified two types of job billings. One was a straight fixed-price contract. The other was a billing based on time spent and materials used to complete the job. Therefore, it initially appeared that the system would have to provide for two primary types of billings. However, Nelson's staff discovered that there were about 15 adaptations of these two types of billings. Nelson wanted to make sure that the billing system would be flexible enough to accommodate each of these adaptations, as well as other possible adaptations that might occur in the future. This was difficult to accomplish, because the functions of the system were not clearly enough defined by the client to enable Nelson's staff to understand the structure and design of all the files. It was not clear whether the accounting firm would be able to put all of the client's contracts on the file. Nelson suggested taking more time with the accountants and marketing people in order to better define the requirements of the system. This would enable the accounting firm to develop the most flexible and useful billing system. However, Marks would not accept this suggestion, citing the need to keep to the schedule.

Bill Nelson wondered what he should do. He did not like the idea of going over the head of the project manager and bringing his concerns to top management. Each time he had approached Perry Marks with his suggestions, however, he was met with resistance. Nelson had become quite concerned that the project was getting too far along without adequate resolution of the problems identified by him and his staff. Engineering Associates was trying to estimate the final implementation date of the system, but Nelson knew this was impractical because of all the unresolved problems.

Bill Nelson suggested to Elliot Wolf that the firm have a quality assurance review program conducted on the job, even though this was outside the scope of services the firm had agreed to offer. Wolf consented, and a consulting partner was brought in from another office to ensure objectivity. The review partner went through a checklist of considerations and identified all the key issues. The project manager did not agree with all the issues or that they presented any problems. However, Nelson tried to get Marks to agree to one of two suggestions:

1. Do more work on defining the functions of the system that were to be implemented rather than uncritically accepting the reports he was receiving from his staff.
2. Put into place the appropriate mechanisms to manage the risk created by the failure to fully identify the functions of the system before proceeding on to subsequent phases of the project.

Marks would not agree to either suggestion. He wanted to continue phasing in the project as if there were no problems. In fact, he wanted a commitment from the accounting firm that various phases of the system would be completed by the dates promised to management. Nelson knew these dates were unrealistic. He felt the project was headed for failure. He did not feel his firm could stand by and support completion by the promised dates. Nelson decided that the next step was to bring the whole issue out in the open and confront top management.

Bill Nelson asked Elliot Wolf to join him in a meeting with the client's top management to discuss the differences of opinion that had developed and the conflicts the accounting firm was experiencing with the project manager. Nelson and Wolf left the meeting believing that top management understood the issues and that the firm's relationship with the project manager would improve in the future. However, while things did improve immediately following the meeting, similar problems and conflicts arose within two weeks. These issues were once again brought to the attention of top management, but the managers' attitude was "We hear what you're saying, but we have to go along with our project manager." During one particular encounter, Marks said to Nelson, "You can pack up your bags and go home if you don't do it my way!"

QUESTIONS

1. Describe the customary relationship between accounting information system consultants and a client for whom they have been hired to design and install an information system. Are there any factors or circumstances in this case that made this kind of relationship more difficult to achieve?
2. Assume that the accounting firm decided to withdraw from the engagement. Would such an action be ethical from a rights or justice point of view?

Compu-View

∎

Compu-View was established in January 1995 by three young engineers in their late twenties. The company was formed as a start-up business to research and develop new computer products. One product in particular holds great promise as a tool to revolutionize the way in which data are formatted. It is a new form of computer networking system that enables entities to transmit data by computer from one location to another and, at the same time, to have audio contact and video contact with the party(ies) to whom the data are being transmitted. The system would be built into a personal computer. It would operate through a connection between the computer and a 46-inch television-type monitor. After placing a telephone call from one location to another, and activating transmission switches at both ends of the connection, data could be transmitted by computer and viewed on one half of the screen while a picture of the party at the other end of the connection would appear on the other half of the screen. This is similar to the split-screen procedure used in televising some sporting events. The attraction of this procedure is that information can be transmitted at the same time that discussions are being held, with the added bonus that the party at the other end of the transmission can be seen. Although other companies are working on combined voice and data transmission over conventional phone lines, Compu-View is believed to be the only company attempting to combine video capabilities with voice and data transmission. The monitor would serve not only as the means of video contact but, additionally, one half of the screen would function as a computer monitor, displaying the transmitted information.

Compu-View is financed by a venture capital firm that provided "seed capital" for the business. The firm is very interested in the features of the networking product being developed by the company. The venture capitalists are encouraged by the fact that Compu-View has recently moved beyond the research stage and into product development. However, they are concerned about the company's inability to line up any customers for the networking product. Because their funds are limited and there are other worthwhile ventures to invest in, the firm has not committed itself to continuing to finance Compu-View beyond mid-1996.

The accounting firm of Harris and Klein LLP was contracted to conduct a review of the December 31, 1995, financial statements of Compu-View. During the early stages of the review, Susan Levin, the manager on the engagement, became aware that Compu-View has been capitalizing all research and development costs instead of expensing them immediately as required by SFAS No. 2, "Accounting for Research and Development Costs." Levin informs Ed Finley, the president of Compu-View, that the company's accounting for these costs is not in accordance with generally accepted accounting principles. As a result, the accounting firm will have to modify its review report to disclose the material departure in a separate paragraph. The firm is not required to verify the effect of the departure on the financial statements, since management has not made that calculation. However, the firm has to disclose this fact in the report. Management's reason for not making the calculation is that the effects of the departure from GAAP are not readily determinable because some of the costs have alternative future uses in other research and development projects, and, therefore, these costs are appropriately capitalized. An example of the review report that will be issued in the absence of other departures appears in Exhibit 1 on page 92.

Finley is concerned about the possible effect of the review report modification on the venture capital firm's willingness to continue its financing of Compu-View. Finley asks Levin whether there are any other options that can be pursued. Levin responds by questioning Finley about the need for a review report and discovers that the venture capital firm did not ask for reviewed financial statements. Levin then outlines the following three options:

1. Submit draft financial statements to Compu-View; each page should be labeled "Draft—subject to changes." The statements would be accompanied by a cover letter stating that, if the firm is required to issue a report in final form as a condition of financing, then it will modify the review report.
2. Complete the engagement and issue a compilation report. (A compilation report, unlike a review report, does not provide any assurances about the statements.)
3. Delay completion of the engagement until an exposure draft of changes to the Statements on Standards for Accounting and Review Services (SSARS) becomes final. This draft exempts assembled financial statements that are for internal use only from the requirements of the SSARS standards. Because Compu-View's statements appear to be intended solely for management's use, reliance on the draft's exemption appears to be a logical option that is consistent with the intent of the proposed standard. Moreover, the engagement fee could be lowered, since the firm would not issue any report on the statements.

Finley initially expresses a preference for either the first or second options because he would like to have a report on hand in case the venture capitalists or other

EXHIBIT 1
Review Report

We have reviewed the accompanying balance sheet of Compu-View as of December 31, 1995, and the related statements of income, retained earnings, and cash flows for the year then ended, in accordance with Statements on Standards for Accounting and Review Services issued by the American Institute of Certified Public Accountants. All information included in these statements is the representation of the management of Compu-View.

A review consists principally of inquiries of company personnel and analytical procedures applied to financial data. It is substantially less broad in scope than an audit in accordance with generally accepted auditing standards, as the objective of an audit is the expression of an opinion regarding the financial statements taken as a whole. Accordingly, we do not express such an opinion.

Based on our review, with the exception of the matter described in the following paragraph, we are not aware of any material modifications that should be made to the accompanying financial statements in order for them to be in conformity with generally accepted accounting principles.

As described in note X to the financial statements, generally accepted accounting principles typically require that research and development costs be expensed against income in the period incurred. Management has informed us that these costs have been capitalized as assets in the balance sheet and that the effects of this departure from generally accepted accounting principles on financial position, results of operations, and cash flows have not been determined.*

*"Compilation and Review of Financial Statements," AR Section 100.40, *AICPA Professional Standards Volume 2,* As of June 1, 1995.

potential investors request such information. Levin points out, however, that if the firm issues a compilation report, it must address the departure from GAAP. An example of a possible compilation report appears in Exhibit 2 on page 93.

Finley expresses his reservations about the compilation report option, although the language explaining the departure is not as troublesome in the compilation report as it is in the review report. He asks Levin to elaborate on the implications of choosing the third option.

Levin explains that the exposure draft is expected to be adopted soon by the Accounting and Review Services Committee. The requirements of the draft become effective immediately upon finalization of the statement. Since Compu-View does not need to have either reviewed or compiled statements, the intent of the draft, as discussed in option 3, above, seems to fit Compu-View's current situation. That is, the financial statements are only needed by management at this time.

At this point Finley expresses his preference for alternatives 1 and 3. He decides to leave the final decision up to Levin and the accounting firm.

EXHIBIT 2
Compilation Report

We have compiled the accompanying balance sheet of Compu-View as of December 31, 1995, and the related statements of income, retained earnings, and cash flows for the year then ended, in accordance with Statements on Standards for Accounting and Review Services issued by the American Institute of Certified Public Accountants.

A compilation is limited to presenting, in the form of financial statements, information that is the representation of management. We have not audited or reviewed the accompanying financial statements and, accordingly, do not express an opinion or any other form of assurance on them. However, we did become aware of a departure from generally accepted accounting principles. This departure is described in the following paragraph.

As disclosed in note 1 to the financial statements, generally accepted accounting principles typically require that research and development costs be expensed against income in the period incurred. Management has informed us that these costs have been capitalized as assets in the balance sheet and that the effects of this departure from generally accepted accounting principles on financial position, results of operations, and cash flows have not been determined.*

*"Compilation and Review of Financial Statements," AR Section 100.40, *AICPA Professional Standards Volume 2,* As of June 1, 1995.

QUESTIONS

1. What are the ethical issues in this case?
2. Given the facts of this case, if you were in Levin's position, what decision would you make?

Financial, Inc.

■

Financial, Inc., is a conglomerate organization offering a variety of services to its customers through three subsidiary companies. The three subsidiary companies consist of a leasing company (S_1), a brokerage company (S_2), and a venture capital company (S_3). Each of the subsidiaries operates as a separate legal entity, incurring its own costs, earning its own revenue, and separately determining its net income. Bonus payments to top corporate officials at each subsidiary are based on the dual factors of individual subsidiary net income and net income for the consolidated entity.

The parent organization (P) is a management consulting entity. It performs several activities that benefit the entire organization, such as payroll services, planning, hiring and firing, the establishment of rates, and the consummation of mergers and acquisitions. The parent company incurred more than $500,000 of costs from these activities during the year ended December 31, 1994. These costs were recorded on the books of the parent entity, without any allocation to the subsidiaries.

George Sheldon is a CPA and the external tax advisor for Financial, Inc. He was reviewing the $640,000 consolidated tax loss amount for 1994 that was determined by the company's accountants. The company had elected to file a consolidated return for the first time in 1994, believing it would be able to derive a tax benefit from offsetting the income of its leasing subsidiary (S_1) against the losses of the other entities. Separate tax returns were filed for each entity in prior tax years.

Sheldon knew that under Internal Revenue Service (IRS) rules, the company could carry back tax losses, within certain limitations, for three tax years and claim a refund for prior taxes paid. Therefore, Financial, Inc., should be able to carry back the $640,000 loss first to 1991, then to 1992, and then to 1993. Any amount that cannot be carried back can be carried forward for 15 years and used to offset future taxable income.[1] Alternatively, the company can elect to carry forward the loss

---

[1]Internal Revenue Code Section 172 (b) (1).

EXHIBIT 1
Financial, Inc.
Schedule of Taxable Income (T/I)
and Tax Paid (T/P)
(000 omitted)
(50% income tax rate)

	1991		1992		1993		Totals	
	T/I	T/P	T/I	T/P	T/I	T/P	T/I	T/P
P	$ 80	$ 40	$ 60	$ 30	$ 40	$ 20	$180	$ 90
S_1	20	10	20	10	20	10	60	30
S_2	120	60	100	50	80	40	300	150
S_3	50	25	30	15	20	10	100	50
Total	$270	$135	$210	$105	$160	$ 80	$640	$320

for 15 years, thereby forgoing the carryback. Exhibit 1 contains the amount of taxable income and the tax paid during the previous three years.

According to tax law, the company was required to segregate the $640,000 tax loss of 1994 by entity in order to carry this amount back and recapture taxes paid since the company had filed separate tax returns during the years 1991–1993. If a specific entity did not have enough taxable income in the prior three years to absorb the full carryback amount, then it could carry forward the remainder and use it to offset future taxable income.[2]

The consolidated tax loss of $640,000 was determined from the following amounts of taxable income (loss) for the year ended December 31, 1994:

P	$(680,000)
S_1	200,000
S_2	(100,000)
S_3	(60,000)
Total	$(640,000)

George Sheldon used the amounts determined by the company and computed the amount of the tax loss for 1994 that could be carried back to each entity. These figures are presented in Exhibit 2 on page 96.

Based on these computations, the company would only be able to use $340,000 as a loss carryback to the previous three tax years. Therefore, it could claim a refund of taxes paid in the amount of $170,000 ($340,000 × .50). The result would be that $300,000 of the tax loss would not be usable by the company in 1994. This amount is determined by deducting the total carryback ($340,000) from the total loss for the year ($640,000).

[2]Internal Revenue Code Income Tax Regulations Section 1.1502-79 (a) (1).

EXHIBIT 2
Financial, Inc.
Schedule of Tax Loss Carryback
(000 omitted)

1994 Income (Loss)		Amount of Carryback			Totals
		1991	1992	1993	
P	$(680)	$ 80*	$60*	$40*	$180
S₁	200	—	—	—	—
S₂	(100)	100	—	—	100
S₃	(60)	50*	10	—	60
Total	$(640)	$230	$70	$40	$340

*These amounts are limited by prior years' taxable incomes.

George Sheldon presented his findings to the management of Financial, Inc. The management's reaction was one of disbelief. The managers could not understand why they were not able to use fully the $640,000 tax loss of the current year to off-set taxes already paid on $640,000 of income in the previous three tax years. The client saw this amount as money that should be available to the company.

The chief executive officer and the chief financial officer of Financial, Inc., asked Sheldon to meet with them to discuss possibilities for better utilization of the tax loss for 1994. They asked Sheldon:

> What if the income or loss for each entity during the current year was different from the amounts we reported. Could that change the extent to which we would be able to use the tax loss *now?* Wouldn't we be better able to utilize our current tax loss if we were able to shift around some of the losses? After all, this wouldn't change the total amount of the loss. We would be merely shifting this amount between entities to maximize our current tax benefit.

Sheldon thought carefully about the request of his client. He was aware of two additional factors. First, the financial statements of Financial, Inc., for the year ended December 31, 1994, were prepared and audited on a consolidated basis. The reported breakdown, by entity, of tax losses for the year was determined by management from the books of Financial, Inc. Sheldon felt there may have been some oversights or inaccuracies in the reported loss figures of each entity, since these amounts had not been audited. Specifically, the $500,000 of costs recorded on the parent company's books might qualify for allocation to the subsidiaries.

Sheldon is also aware that any claimed tax refund that is over $1 million is likely to be audited by the IRS, because it exceeds the threshold for review by the Joint Committee on Internal Revenue Taxation. The figures submitted by management justify a refund of at least $170,000—and perhaps as much as $320,000. If Sheldon decides to review the $500,000, and he determines that certain common costs incurred by the parent entity probably should be allocated to each of the subsidiaries, then he will feel justified in recommending the allocation. Moreover, he can maximize the potential tax benefit for his client by taking an aggressive position and allocating the costs in amounts that produce adjusted taxable losses for 1994 that equal the taxable amounts reported for 1991–1993, as presented in Exhibit 1. Since the IRS is not likely to audit the amended returns for the prior three years, Sheldon feels more comfortable about doing this.

QUESTIONS

1. Evaluate George Sheldon's reasoning, based on the statements in the last paragraph of the case. Is it consistent with ethical reasoning? At what stage of moral development does Sheldon appear to be?

2. According to AICPA's *Statement on Responsibilities in Tax Practice No. 1,* a CPA should not recommend a tax return position to a client unless the CPA has a "good faith belief that the position has a realistic possibility of being sustained administratively or judicially on its merits if challenged." Do you believe that this standard is consistent with encouraging the kind of ethical decision making discussed in the second section of the book? Can you restate the standard so that it serves as a better tool for achieving this goal?

Cubbies Cable

■

Ernie Binks is a big baseball fan, so it is quite natural for him, at a time like this, to recall a phrase attributed to "Yogi Berra": It was deja vu all over again.

Binks is the partner in charge of the Cubbies Cable audit for the accounting firm of Santos & Williams LLP. He is involved in a second dispute in three years with client management. The first dispute concerned the capitalization of cable construction costs that the client wanted to expense. The current dispute concerns the proper recording of profit on a sale-leaseback transaction in the fiscal year-end September 30, 1995, financial statements. Binks was able to convince top management that the accounting firm's position was correct on the capitalization issue. However, he wonders about the current situation—if for no other reason than that he knows the "culture" of the firm and its approach to disputes with clients. The firm's approach is that "You have to let the client win one somewhere along the line or you may lose that client." Binks will meet with John Kessinger, the advisory partner on the Cubbies Cable audit, to discuss the current dispute with client management. Prior to doing that, Binks wants to review the details of the first dispute and the facts of the current one, as well.

Binks starts by reviewing a memorandum in the workpapers from the September 30, 1993, audit. The document summarizes the facts of the first dispute. This memo is presented in Exhibit 1 on page 99.

Accounting for the Sale and Leaseback

Binks now focuses on the current dispute with Don Zummer, the president of Cubbies Cable, and Jim Fry, the controller of the company. On September 1, 1995, the company entered into a sale-leaseback agreement with the owners of a large garden apartment complex (the "complex"). Under the agreement, Cubbies sold the cable system and then leased it back from the complex to supply cable services to subscribers. Part of the purpose of the sale-leaseback transaction is to provide some

EXHIBIT 1
Memo on Capitalization of Cable Equipment
November 30, 1993

1. Cubbies Cable is a locally owned cable television company that services the neighborhoods in Chicago that surround Wrigley Field, the home of the Chicago Cubs. Cubbies Cable was incorporated as a closely held company in 1991. We have audited the company's financial statements since September 30, 1992. The audited statements are used by Chicago First National Bank in granting short-term loans to Cubbies Cable. In particular, the company has a debt covenant agreement with the bank that obligates Cubbies to maintain a specified level of liquidity as indicated by the working capital and "quick" ratios. Tension exists between the firm and top management about maintaining required liquidity levels. It seems that top management is motivated to maintain or exceed those levels—even if it has to adopt questionable accounting practices to achieve this result. One such instance occurred during the current audit of the September 30, 1993, financial statements, as described in item 2, below.

2. During the *prematurity period** from October 1, 1991, through September 30, 1993, the client constructed its cable system and earned some revenue from subscriber services. Cable services were offered only to single-dwelling homes in the wealthier areas around Wrigley Field in order to ensure a steady stream of collectible revenue.

A difference of opinion arose over the proper accounting for cable construction costs. The client wanted to expense some costs and capitalize others, with no conceptual basis to support its position. We suspect that the client wanted to reduce net income so that it could minimize income taxes and the resulting cash outflows. Two different types of costs were involved:

a. Cable television plant: Costs associated with constructing the *cable television plant* and providing cable service include *head-end costs, cable,* and *drop costs.* The client wanted to expense some of these costs and capitalize others. However, Statement of Financial Accounting Standards No. 51, "Financial Reporting by Cable Television Companies," requires that cable television plant costs incurred during the prematurity period be capitalized in full. John Kessinger and I had protracted discussions with Cubbies Cable regarding this issue, and we were able to convince the client that its accounting procedure was not in accordance with generally accepted accounting principles.

b. Interest costs: The client initially expensed some costs and capitalized others based on the consistency of this approach with the treatment of costs incurred on the associated cable television plant. We convinced the client to change its accounting by reference to SFAS No. 51. This Statement requires application of SFAS No. 34, "Capitalization of Interest Cost," to interest costs incurred during the construction of an asset. The application of paragraphs 13 and 14 of SFAS No. 34 to the client's situation requires that interest costs incurred during the prematurity period be capitalized in full by applying the

---

*See definitions in Exhibit 3, on page 104, for all italicized words.

(continued)

EXHIBIT 1 *(continued)*
Memo on Capitalization of Cable Equipment
November 30, 1993

---

interest capitalization rate to the average amount of accumulated expenditures for the asset during the period. The purpose of this procedure is to capitalize the amount of interest costs incurred during the prematurity period that theoretically could have been avoided if expenditures for construction of the cable television plant had not been made.

---

needed financing so that the cable company can convert its cable system from the old coaxial cable to the newer, but more expensive, fiber-optic cable. The terms of the sale-leaseback agreement are summarized in Exhibit 2.

EXHIBIT 2
Sale-Leaseback Agreement

Cost of the cable	$1,000,000
Estimated useful life	20 years
Estimated residual value	n/a
Sale price to the complex	$3,000,000

Terms of the leaseback:

Leaseback Period

- Five-year periods, renewable three times, for a total of 20 years.
- Renewal subject to approval of the buyer-lessor.
- Seller-lessee can sell its rights to the cable at any time, but purchaser company assumes all obligations under this lease agreement, including payments to the complex.

Leaseback Rentals

- Monthly payments to the complex based on revenue received from cable subscribers.
- 20% of monthly subscription revenue retained by Cubbies Cable.
- 80% of monthly subscription revenue payable by Cubbies to the complex for a maximum of 20 years (subject to leaseback period terms and above provisions).

Other

- Lessee incremental borrowing rate = 10%.
- There are a total of 400 apartment units in the complex.

The difference of opinion with Zummer and Fry is over the $2 million gain on the sale of the cable system. Top management's position is that it constitutes revenue that should be recognized in full in the September 30, 1995, income statement. Binks's position is that this amount should be deferred and recognized over the 20-year leaseback period as an adjustment of the rental expense payments that will be made to the complex based on subscriber revenue. For example, at 100% occupancy and 100% cable subscription levels, Cubbies would pay rental of $16,000 each month, using the historical average monthly cable service fee of $50 for each subscriber (400 units × $50 fee = $20,000 revenue × $.80 to the complex = $16,000). This amount would be offset by $8,333, the portion of the deferred revenue to be recognized as revenue each month ($2,000,000/20 years × 1/12 = $8,333).

Binks believes that the company's position is motivated by its need for financing beyond that provided by the sale-leaseback transaction. Together, the cost to Cubbies Cable for expanding its service area throughout Chicago and the significant outlay required to convert the system to fiber-optic cable have drained the company's resources. Binks knows that the company plans to take the 1995 audited financial statements and apply for long-term financing at Chicago First National Bank. The likelihood of securing the needed financing is greater if the company maximizes its net income and improves its leveraged position.

Binks now turns to the authoritative support for his position. According to SFAS No. 28, "Accounting for Sales with Leasebacks," which amends SFAS No. 13, "Accounting for Leases," the seller-lessee should defer the profit on a sale-leaseback transaction if the seller retains substantially all of the use of the property through the leaseback. Binks believes that Cubbies Cable does have the right to use the property, whereas Zummer and Fry contend that the cable company's rights to use the property are subject to the continued lease agreement between Cubbies and the complex. Since that agreement can be broken at the end of the first five years or upon sale of the company's rights to another company, top management's interpretation of SFAS No. 28 is that all of the gain should be recognized immediately. Specifically, management identified paragraph 3 of SFAS No. 28, which supersedes paragraph 33 of SFAS No. 13, as support for Cubbies' position:

SFAS No. 28, "Accounting for
Sales with Leasebacks" (Paragraph 3)

If the seller-lessee relinquishes the right to substantially all of the remaining use of the property sold (retaining only a minor portion of such use), the sale and leaseback should be accounted for as separate transactions, based on their respective terms.

Binks tried to persuade Zummer and Fry that, even if their interpretation of *substantially all* and *minor* were correct, application of these concepts to Cubbies' sale-leaseback transaction would still be impossible. This is because SFAS No. 28 defines these terms in the context of the capital lease criteria of SFAS No. 13. To apply these criteria, Cubbies would have to calculate the present value of the future lease payments. Since those payments constitute *contingent rentals* under

SFAS No. 29, they should be excluded from minimum lease payments, thereby making that concept irrelevant to Cubbies' situation. Binks identified the following to support his position:

SFAS No. 29, "Determining Contingent Rentals"
(Paragraphs 1, 2, and 11)

Only amounts based on a measurable factor existing at the inception of the lease are included in minimum lease payments. Lease payments that depend on a factor like future sales volume of a leased facility are contingent rentals in their entirety and are excluded from minimum lease payments because future sales do not exist at the inception of the lease. Contingent rentals should be included in the determination of income as accruable.

Binks likened the example of future sales volume of a leased facility to the future rental of apartments at the complex and the related demand for cable service. There is no guarantee of a determinable rental income level or demand for cable television services. The accuracy of any attempted calculation could not be objectively determined. Moreover, Binks emphasized that, if the complex decides to change cable television service providers, as is possible under the lease agreement, then the lease payments to the complex (which are based on contingent rentals) would terminate. Cubbies would then come to an agreement with the new provider for the sale of their rights to the cable. Therefore, the company has, in essence, retained the right to *substantially all* of the property.

It is this last point that created the most tension between Binks and Zummer. In particular, Zummer asked Binks what would happen with the remaining deferred revenue if the complex terminated the lease agreement at the end of five years or if Cubbies were to be taken over by a larger cable company. Zummer emphasized that the latter is a distinct possibility if Cubbies cannot get the needed financing to keep up with technological changes. Additionally, there is increased competition in the television cable market because of the recent deregulation by Congress. Binks informed Zummer that, in such a case, the remainder of the deferred revenue would then be recognized as revenue in its entirety in the year that the relationship with the complex terminates.

At this point Zummer, who is known for his temper, becomes quite angry. He reminds Binks that he gave in on the last dispute over the capitalization of cable installation costs. He tells Binks that he has no intention of giving in on this issue, and that Binks should discuss the matter with Kessinger.

Having reviewed the facts of the current dispute with top management, Binks is now ready to meet with Kessinger. Binks is not looking forward to this meeting. He knows that the firm recently lost an important client because of a disagreement with the president. The pressure is on to either compromise with clients when there are differences of opinion or go along with the client's position whenever there are gray areas in interpreting accounting standards.

During the meeting, Binks briefs Kessinger on the sale-leaseback transaction. Kessinger asks Binks whether there may be a compromise position to take with the client. In particular, he asks whether some of the gain on sale can be recognized in the current year and the rest of it deferred and matched against rental expense on the leaseback. They discuss the application of SFAS No. 28 as it relates to this issue. According to the statement:

> If the seller retains more than a minor part but less than substantially all of the use of the property through the leaseback and the profit on the sale exceeds the present value of the minimum lease payments called for by the leaseback for an operating lease, . . . that excess would be recognized as profit at the date of the sale.

Binks tells Kessinger about the problem that he identified in his discussions with Zummer and Fry. That is, the present value of the minimum lease payments cannot be reliably determined because of uncertainty about future occupancy levels, the number of cable service subscribers, and the number of subscription packages. Binks concludes by saying that the total amount of profit on the sale should be deferred and taken into income as an adjustment to the contingent rental expense payments.

Kessinger understands the reasons for Binks's position, but he points out that this matter is not so clear-cut. It can be argued that the sale-leaseback meets the "greater than minor but less than substantially all" criterion for partial recognition. Conceptually, then, there should be some profit recognition in 1995. However, no profit recognition is possible, because the required calculation cannot be made. Therefore, Kessinger wants to support the client on this matter. In this way, if the cable system is sold or the complex decides to hire a new cable provider, Cubbies will not have to write off the remaining deferred revenue. It is desirable to avoid this write-off because a lump sum adjustment to income could have a misleading effect on the financial statements. Binks and Kessinger end the discussion by setting up a meeting at 9 A.M. on the following day to discuss the matter with Ron Hundley, the managing partner of the firm.

Binks is quite perplexed at this point. Although he recognizes that, in some cases, generally accepted accounting principles are not always clear, he does not believe this is one of those situations. Moreover, he wonders about the client's motives in taking a rather aggressive position on revenue recognition. Binks contemplates his options—either to go along with the client's position (the option supported by Kessinger) or to maintain his own position when he and Kessinger meet with Hundley. It is at this point that he thinks about another "Yogi-ism": "When you come to a fork in the road, take it."

QUESTIONS

1. Using Kohlberg's cognitive development model, describe the various levels of moral reasoning of each of the main characters in this case: Don Zummer, Ernie Binks, and John Kessinger. What virtues are represented by the position each takes?

EXHIBIT 3
Definitions of Terms from SFAS Nos. 28, 29, and 51

SFAS No. 28, "Accounting for Sales with Leasebacks" (Paragraph 3a)

Substantially All and Minor. The phrase *substantially all and minor* is used in the context of the concepts underlying the classification criteria of SFAS No. 13. In that context, a test based on the 90% recovery criterion of Statement No. 13 could be used as a guideline. That is, if the present value of a reasonable amount of rental for the leaseback represents 10% or less of the fair value of the asset sold, the seller-lessee could be presumed to have transferred to the purchaser-lessor the right to substantially all of the remaining use of the property sold, and the seller-lessee could be presumed to have retained only a minor portion of such use.

SFAS No. 29, "Determining Contingent Rentals" (Paragraph 11)

Contingent Rentals. These represent the increases and decreases in lease payments that result from changes occurring subsequent to the inception of the lease in the factors (other than the passage of time) on which lease payments are based. For example, lease payments that depend on a factor directly related to the future use of the leased property, such as sales volume during the lease term, are contingent rentals and should be excluded from minimum lease payments.

SFAS No. 51, "Financial Reporting by Cable Television Companies" (Paragraph 17)

Cable Television Plant. This refers to the cable television system required to render services to subscribers and includes the following equipment:

Head-End. The equipment used to receive television signals, including the studio facilities required to transmit the programs to subscribers.

Cable. This consists of cable and amplifiers placed on utility poles or underground that maintain the quality of the signal to subscribers.

Drops. This consists of the hardware that provides access to the main cable in order to bring the signal from the main cable to the subscriber's television set, and devices to block channels.

Converters and Descramblers. These are devices attached to the subscriber's television sets when more than 12 channels are provided, such as Pay-per-View programming or two-way communication.

Prematurity Period. This refers to the period of time during which the cable television system is partially under construction and partially in service. It begins with the first earned subscriber revenue and ends with the completion of the first major construction period or achievement of a specified, predetermined subscriber level at which no additional investment will be required, other than that for cable television plant.

---

2. Assume you are in Ernie Binks's position. You have decided to stand by your judgment that all of the profit on the initial sale should be deferred and amortized over the leaseback period. What would you do if, at tomorrow's meeting, Hundley decides that the firm should support the client on the revenue-recognition matter?

Classic Silk Clothiers, Inc.

■

"How can I bypass top management on this issue? After all, the audit committee of the board of directors probably would not have backed our nomination as external auditors without the support of Stu Davis (the chief executive officer)."

These comments were made by Glen Wellman, the partner in charge of the Classic Silk Clothiers audit. Wellman was discussing a sensitive matter with Ken Jamison, the managing partner of the Philadelphia office of Hughes & Fisher LLP. Jamison recommended that Wellman disclose his findings directly to Fred Garrison, the chairperson of the audit committee, without first discussing them with the CEO. Wellman does not agree. He is afraid that, if he does so, Davis will accuse him of being disloyal. Moreover, Davis may then decide not to recommend the firm to assist Classic Silk in the design and installation of its new management information system. Wellman has been working for three years to get this lucrative contract. He knows how important it is for new partners, like himself, to bring in new business. He does not want to do anything that might upset Davis and turn him against the firm.

Classic Silk Clothiers is a publicly owned company that manufactures silk clothing from fabrics provided by textile mills outside Philadelphia. The clothing is sold to upscale stores in the wealthier areas of the city and across the United States. Classic aggressively competes with three other wholesalers for retail customers. An important part of the business strategy is to "wine and dine" buyers for these stores in the hope of influencing their final decision. At Classic Silk it is not unusual to find members of top management engaged in this type of travel and entertainment activity. In particular, Larry Ames, the vice president of marketing, travels around the country in search of new retail outlets.

The audit committee at Classic Silk Clothiers has a variety of responsibilities related to financial reporting, internal controls, and corporate governance. Among other things, the audit committee has oversight responsibility for officers' expenses and perquisites, including use of corporate assets.

Glen Wellman was approached two weeks ago by Garrison, who asked whether the firm had audited the travel and entertainment account. Specifically, Garrison asked Wellman what the firm does about the travel and entertainment expenditures of the top officers. Wellman pointed out that these are included in the population that is sampled. However, the firm does not necessarily review all of these expenditures. Garrison said that he wants the auditors to investigate, on a separate basis, all of the time reports and supporting documentation for all of the travel and entertainment expenses for the officers for the past year. Garrison told Wellman to report the findings of the investigation directly to him. Wellman was surprised by this, because in the past, the audit committee has not taken an active role in such matters.

The auditors found several questionable items in their audit of travel and entertainment. No one item was material to net income and only two officers are involved in questionable practices. One is Larry Ames, who has a habit of taking his wife with him on cross-country trips, especially to San Francisco. Ames includes his wife's travel, meals, and entertainment costs in his expense report. On more than one occasion, he and his wife have taken a side trip after business was completed, and he charged the company for their personal expenditures.

The internal auditors were contacted and admitted knowing about these items. However, they have not taken any action because Stu Davis personally approved the expenditures, as required by company policy. It seems that Davis believes these expenditures are acceptable business expenses. Ames often invites both the buyer and the buyer's spouse to dinner. Since many of the buyers are women, Ames feels that it is important for his wife to accompany him on business trips. The side trips do not occur regularly, and Davis feels that these are acceptable "perks" of the job.

The other officer who is involved in questionable practices is Don Matthis. Matthis is the vice president for human resources. Among other things, he helps to entertain out-of-town buyers who come to the Philadelphia area. For example, his duties include making the arrangements for these guests to attend events at the Philadelphia Spectrum Sports Arena. The company owns the rights to an eight-seat skybox for all home games of the Philadelphia 76ers professional basketball team. It costs the company $41,000 for the 41 home games. When the seats are not being used to entertain buyers or potential buyers, Matthis will frequently use the seats for himself or will give passes to them to other employees of the company.

One benefit of owning season tickets is that the holder gets first option on buying skybox tickets for the basketball playoffs, should the 76ers qualify. Also, the company can buy tickets for special events at the Spectrum. For example, there was a $1,000 expenditure during the year for tickets to the Hootie and the Blowfish concert at the Spectrum. It seems that several youthful buyers were in town that night and Matthis thought it was a good idea to take them to the concert.

Wellman will meet with Garrison tomorrow to discuss the audit findings of the travel and entertainment accounts. Wellman wants to first inform Davis about his findings. However, Ken Jamison cautioned against doing this, noting that Garrison told Wellman to report directly to him. Jamison does not want to upset either the audit committee or Garrison, who might have good reasons to suspect Davis and other officers of improprieties.

QUESTIONS

1. Considering the limited facts of this case, do you think that the travel and entertainment expenditures of Larry Ames, in particular, and the skybox expenditures are proper business expenses? What are the implications of these expenses for the audit of Classic Silk Clothiers? Do you think the IRS would allow part or all of these expenditures as income tax deductions? Why or why not?
2. Glen Wellman seems to believe that the firm has a loyalty obligation to Stu Davis, the chief executive officer, because Davis was instrumental in the firm's selection as the independent auditors. Also, Davis will be instrumental in choosing a firm to do the management information systems work. Ken Jamison, on the other hand, seems to emphasize the audit committee's oversight role for internal controls and corporate governance. To whom do the external auditors owe their ultimate allegiance? Is it to the management of Classic Silk Clothiers, to the audit committee of the board of directors, or to some other group? How does the perceived loyalty obligation relate to the propriety of Wellman's informing Davis of his findings before meeting with Fred Garrison?

CASES

INTERNAL REPORTING

Whistle-Blowing and the Professional

■

This case describes an actual situation where a public employee blew the whistle on wrongdoing in a state agency. The names have been changed, but the facts are as stated below.

Barbara Reznik joined the Department of Transportation as an architect in 1982. In 1988, after six years on the job, Reznik told her superiors about what she regarded as fraud and corruption in the department's purchasing and leasing practices. Reznik claimed that officials were accepting kickbacks for awarding contracts to certain companies and contractors. She noted that this practice was costing the taxpayers millions of dollars.

Reznik waited several months for a response to her charges, but none was forthcoming. Finally, she approached her superiors once again, informing them that she intended to report the problems to outside authorities. Within one month, the department began an investigation of Reznik's long-distance telephone use covering a 2 1/2-year period. They found one improper 13-cent phone call among the thousands of calls and referred the violation to the county district attorney. The next month, the department began investigating Reznik's use of sick leave. An audit found that she failed to attend a therapy session for a leg injury she suffered on the job. Reznik said she missed the appointment because her car brakes failed, and that she had called her supervisor from the repair shop to explain the problem. Reznik was subsequently fired from her job and indicted.

Barbara Reznik decided to sue under the state's Whistleblower Act. The law prohibits retaliation against public employees who exercise good faith in reporting official wrongdoing. The state's supreme court has ruled that "whistleblowers act in good faith as long as they truly believe that something illegal is going on and that their belief was reasonable in light of the employee's training and experience."

A public employee who reports a violation of law and is retaliated against or experiences discrimination can file a suit against the governmental body for actual and punitive damages and/or reinstatement, lost wages, court costs, and legal fees. A supervisor who has wrongfully fired or suspended a whistle-blower from a public agency can be fined up to $1,000. The burden of proof in such cases is on the whistle-blower who sues the government.

Shortly after Reznik initiated legal action, the district attorney offered to drop the criminal proceedings against her if Reznik would drop her lawsuit. She refused to do so. Ultimately, the charges against Reznik were dismissed.

Reznik was successful in her lawsuit and was awarded $3.5 million in personal damages, $10 million in punitive damages, and $160,000 in attorney fees. That was in 1991. The state appealed the decision at both the appellate and the supreme court levels, and lost each time. Now, four years after the initial decision, the state owes Reznik $20.4 million, because interest accrues at the rate of about $4,800 per day.

Reznik has not been able to collect her award from the state, however, because the Whistleblower Act requires that the legislature first fund the amount in its budget. The legislature has been reluctant to do so, since most members view the award as excessive. The position of many of the legislators seems to be that it is not in the public interest to divert such a large amount of money from funds available to meet the needs of the public. However, a compromise was eventually reached between those legislators supporting payment and those against it. The offer is to pay Reznik only the $3.5 million awarded for personal damages. Reznik refuses, stating that, as a matter of principle, she believes that the legislature should pay the full $20.4 million.

Reznik has now been unemployed for four years. She has received one or two low-level clerical job offers, but has been unable to secure a position similar in responsibility to the one she had at the Department of Transportation. She has turned down the clerical job offers, knowing that she would only accept such employment temporarily—that is, until she receives payment from the state. At that time, she would once again seek a more suitable position or simply retire.

Reznik owes $4.6 million to her lawyers for services performed after the initial lawsuit. She also borrowed $1 million from a financier. She is currently living in a trailer and often has to rely on friends for meals and other financial support.

QUESTIONS

1. Do you think that Barbara Reznik has a right to expect the state to pay the full $20.4 million? How does the "public interest" enter into your assessment of the appropriateness of the state's offer? If you were in Reznik's position, would you accept the offer? Be sure to incorporate ethical reasoning into your responses.

2. Notwithstanding the existence of the Whistleblower Act, assume that Reznik is a CPA working in the accounting office at the Department of Transportation, and the fraud that she identifies concerns financial statement items. Would you advise Reznik to blow the whistle on the financial wrongdoing? What if she were a CMA or CIA? What ethical and professional considerations are relevant in making such a decision, and what action would you advise?

Supreme Designs, Inc.

∎

Supreme Designs, Inc., is a small manufacturing company located in Detroit, Michigan. There are three stockholders of the company—Gary Hoffman, Ed Webber, and John Sullivan. Hoffman manages the business. Webber and Sullivan do most of the sales work, and they cultivate potential customers for Supreme Designs. Hoffman recently hired his daughter, Janet, to manage the office. Janet has successfully managed a small clothing boutique in downtown Detroit for the past eight years. She sold the shop to a regional department store that wanted to expand its operation. Gary Hoffman hopes that his daughter will take over as an owner in a few years when he reaches retirement age.

Janet Hoffman is given complete control over the payroll, and she approves disbursements, signs checks, and reconciles the general ledger cash account to the bank statement balance. Previously, the bookkeeper was the only employee with such authority. However, the bookkeeper recently left the company, and Gary Hoffman needs someone he can trust to be in charge of these sensitive operations. Hoffman did ask his daughter to hire someone as soon as possible to help with these and other accounting functions. Janet Hoffman hired Kevin Greenberg shortly thereafter, based on a friend's recommendation.

Greenberg is a relatively inexperienced accountant. He graduated from college with a Bachelor's Degree in Accounting 16 months ago, and since then he has been working for a local accounting firm. However, Greenberg's career goal is to work in private industry, and someday he hopes to own and operate a small business. First, he wants to become a CMA. Therefore, he jumped at the opportunity to work for Supreme Designs.

On April 22, 1995, about one year after hiring Kevin Greenberg, Janet Hoffman discovers that she needs surgery. Even though the procedure is a fairly common one, with little risk of complications, Janet is expected to miss between two and three weeks of work. She asks Greenberg to approve vouchers for payment and present them to her father, who will write the checks during her absence from

114

the company. Janet previously discussed this with her father, and they both agreed that Greenberg is now ready to assume additional responsibilities.

The bank statement for April arrives on May 3, 1995. Janet did not tell Greenberg to reconcile the cash account balance to the bank statement. However, Greenberg decides to do it anyway, as a favor to Janet, who is not expected to return to the office for at least another week.

Although everything appears to be in order, Greenberg is not sure what to make of the fact that Janet approved and signed five checks payable to herself for the same amount during the month of April. Each check appears in numerical sequence, once in about every 10 checks. Greenberg is surprised by this because the payroll is supposed to be processed only once a month. In fact, he found only one canceled check for each of the other employees, including himself.

Curiosity gets the best of Greenberg, and he decides to trace the checks paid to Janet to the cash disbursements journal. He looks for supporting documentation. During his review, Greenberg notices that each of the five checks has been coded to a different account and that, in each case, there is no supporting voucher or other documentation for the transaction. He decides to expand his search by reviewing the bank statements for the first three months of the year. For the four months, including April, Greenberg identifies 20 checks made out to Janet, each for the same amount. The disbursements have been coded to 10 different accounts, such as supplies, rent, salaries, travel, and miscellaneous expenses. Individually, each of these checks is not large enough to be material to net income. The amounts are material in the aggregate, however, assuming the practice occurs all year long.

At this point Greenberg pauses and starts to consider the consequences of his actions. He wonders whether he should have opened the bank statement in the first place. He is concerned that he may have uncovered the fraudulent use of company resources. If so, how should he handle the situation? Alternatively, he wonders whether there is anything wrong with the owner's daughter withdrawing funds from a business that is family owned?

QUESTION

What should be the issues of concern to Kevin Greenberg in deciding on a course of action? What role, if any, should the ethical standards of the accounting profession play in his decision? What would you do if you were Kevin Greenberg? Be sure to support your position with ethical reasoning.

Sweat Hog Construction Company

■

Ever since the economy of southern California began to decline, in early 1991, Sweat Hog Construction Company has been more aggressive in seeking out new business opportunities. One such opportunity is the Computer Assistance Vocational Training School. It has contracted for a new 1-million-square-foot facility in Rancho Cucamonga, California. Computer Assistance trains computer programmers for jobs in business and government. It is the largest computer training school on the West Coast.

Gabe Kotter is the passive owner of Sweat Hog Construction. The company began operating in 1978, when Kotter hired Michael Woodman to be the president of the company. Sweat Hog Construction is a family-owned business that has been very successful as a mechanical contractor of heating, ventilation, and air-conditioning systems. However, the economic downturn of the 1990s put pressure on the company to diversify its operations. Although it made a profit in 1994, the company's net income for the year was 50% lower than in previous years. As a result of these factors, the company decided to expand into plumbing and electrical contract work.

In March 1995, Sweat Hog successfully bid for the Computer Assistance job. The company bid low in order to secure the $3 million contract that is expected to be completed by June 30, 1996. Woodman knows that the company has little margin for error on the contract. The estimated gross margin of 11.5% is on the low side of historical margins, which have been between 10 to 15% on heating, ventilation, and air-conditioning contracts. Since it is a fixed-price contract, the company will have to absorb any cost overruns.

The Computer Assistance contract is an important one for Sweat Hog Construction. It represents about 20% of the average annual revenues for the past five years. Moreover, First National Bank of California has been pressuring the company to speed up its interest payments on a $2 million term loan payable to the bank that is renewable on March 15, 1996. The company has been late in five of its last six monthly payments. The main reason is that some of the company's customers have been paying their bills later than usual because of tight economic conditions. However, the company expects to get back on the right track very soon after the Computer Assistance job begins.

Everything started out well on the contract. For the quarter ended June 30, 1995, Sweat Hog had an estimated cumulative gross profit of $75,000 on the contract under the percentage-of-completion method. This represents a 20% gross margin. Costs started to increase during the September quarter and, even though the cumulative gross margin decreased to 10%, it was still within projected amounts. Unfortunately, the $54,000 estimated gross profit for the nine months ended December 31, 1995, represents only a 3% gross margin for the first year of the contract. Exhibit 1 contains cost data, billings, and collections for the year.

Vinny Barbarino is the controller of Sweat Hog Construction. Barbarino knows that cash collections on the Computer Assistance project have been slowing down—in part, because the company is behind schedule—and tension has developed between the company and Computer Assistance. He decides to contact Juan Epstein, general manager for the project. Epstein informs Barbarino that the tension between the company and Computer Assistance escalated recently when Epstein informed top management of Computer Assistance that the electrical work may not be completed by the June 30, 1996, deadline. If the facility does not open as scheduled for the summer months, Computer Assistance may be required to return deposits from students. Consequently, it may lose out on the revenue that is projected for the July and August summer term.

Woodman calls for a meeting with Epstein and Barbarino on February 6, 1996, to discuss the Computer Assistance contract. Woodman knows that Sweat Hog's external auditors will begin their audit of the December 31, 1995, year-end financial statements in two weeks. Woodman wants to make sure the problems with the contract have been corrected. He asks Barbarino to bring him up to date on the recent cost increases on the contract.

EXHIBIT 1
Sweat Hog Construction Company
Computer Assistance Contract
Year Ended December 31, 1995

	Quarter Ending		
	June 30	Sept. 30	Dec. 31
Costs to date	$ 300,000	$ 900,000	$1,740,000
Estimated costs to complete	2,100,000	1,800,000	1,170,000
Progress billings each quarter	250,000	600,000	950,000
Cash collections each quarter	150,000	350,000	400,000

Barbarino informs Woodman that the internal job cost data indicate that $420,000 was incurred for the month of January 1996. About 10% of the work was completed during that month. Barbarino emphasizes that this is consistent with recent trend data that indicate the estimated costs to complete the contract have been significantly understated. In fact, for the quarter ended December 31, 1995, the company lost approximately $46,000 on the contract, although there is a cumulative gross margin of about $54,000 for 1995. However, this cumulative margin represents only 3% of revenue, and the gross margin percentage is declining. Barbarino analyzed the cost data in preparation for the meeting. He estimates that total costs on the contract may be as high as $4.2 million. He recommends that the $1.17 million estimate to complete the contract at December 31, 1995, should be increased by at least $1 million.

Woodman is stunned by this information. He cannot understand how the company got into this predicament. The company has consistently made profits on its contracts, and there has never before been any tension with clients. The timing is particularly troublesome, since First National Bank is expecting audited financial statements by March 1, 1996. Woodman asks Epstein whether he agrees with Barbarino's assessment about the anticipated higher level of future costs. Epstein hesitates, at first, but he eventually admits to the likelihood of the cost overruns. He points out that the workers are not as skilled with electrical work as they are with heating, ventilation, and air-conditioning work. Consequently, some degree of learning is taking place on the job.

Woodman dismisses Epstein at this point and asks Barbarino what would happen if the company reports the estimated costs at December 31, 1995, without any adjustments. Woodman emphasizes that the company would make the necessary adjustments in the first quarter of 1996, and gross profit on the contract with Computer Assistance ultimately will be correct. This approach will enable the company to renew its loan and will give it some time to rethink its business strategy. However, Barbarino is not comfortable with this approach, since the profit on the contract for the nine months ended December 31, 1995, would be significantly overstated. He points out that the auditors are likely to question the low cost estimates. Woodman becomes a bit irritated with Barbarino at this point. He tells Barbarino that the bank is not likely to renew the company's $2 million loan if the statements reflect what Barbarino suggests. He concludes by stating:

> The auditors have never been a problem before. I do not expect any problems from them on this issue either, given the current economic situation and the competition for professional accounting services.

QUESTIONS

1. What are Vinny Barbarino's options in this case? Would Barbarino have any special obligations if he were a CPA or CMA?
2. Using the tools of ethical analysis described in the second section of the book, evaluate the ethics of each option and its effects on the stakeholders. What should Barbarino do?

Borwood Leveraged Buyout

■

INTRODUCTION

It has been said that managers can manipulate short-term reported earnings by choosing certain accounting methods and by selecting the timing of some nonoperating events, such as the sale of excess assets or the placement of gains or losses into a particular reporting period.[1] This case deals with the ethics of recording an asset at a lower amount than may be justifiable under generally accepted accounting principles in order to minimize future depreciation charges and maximize net income.

BACKGROUND

On January 2, 1995, Ellen Borwood, the sole stockholder and chief executive officer of Borwood Printing Corporation, agreed to sell all of her stock in Borwood to Jim Westford, a wealthy investor from Florida, for $5 million in cash. To effect the acquisition, Westford organized a shell corporation, Borwood Acquisition Corporation ("NEWCO"), which would purchase all of the stock of Borwood Printing ("OLDCO"). NEWCO financed the entire purchase price of $5 million through an unrelated third-party finance company. On the date of the acquisition, OLDCO was immediately merged into NEWCO so that OLDCO ceased to exist and NEWCO remained as the sole surviving corporation.

Westford is the president and sole stockholder of NEWCO. Westford would like the company to go public at some point in the future, although he does not expect this to happen for at least five years. One of Westford's first actions is to hire David

[1]Bruns, William J., Jr., and K. A. Merchant, "The Dangerous Morality of Managing Earnings," *Management Accounting,* August 1990, pp. 22–25.

EXHIBIT 1
Borwood Printing Corporation
Premerger Balance Sheet
January 2, 1995

Assets		Liabilities and Equity	
Cash	$ 100,000	Accounts payable	$ 700,000
Accounts receivable	300,000	Accrued liabilities	25,000
Inventory	800,000	Equipment notes	
Printing equipment (net		payable to bank	2,000,000
of accumulated depr.)	3,000,000		
Other equipment	200,000	Common stock	100,000
		Retained earnings	1,575,000
		Total liabilities	
Total assets	**$4,400,000**	**and equity**	**$4,400,000**

Lewis, who is a CPA and a CMA, to be in charge of the accounting function. Lewis is given the premerger balance sheet for OLDCO that appears in Exhibit 1.

ACCOUNTING ISSUES

Lewis researches the accounting literature in order to determine whether any guidelines exists on accounting for the leveraged buyout (LBO). He discovers that Issue No. 88-16 of the Financial Accounting Standards Board Emerging Issues Task Force applies the concepts of APB Opinion (APBO) #16 to the transaction.

According to Issue No. 88-16, a new basis of accounting should be established for the assets and liabilities, because there is a complete change in control of the voting interest of Borwood Printing. The transaction is similar to a purchase-business combination. Therefore, APBO #16 requires that NEWCO allocate the cost of acquiring OLDCO to the fair values of the net assets at the date of acquisition. The excess cost of acquiring OLDCO over the fair values should be recorded as goodwill. The amount of goodwill should be amortized against earnings in equal amounts over the period that is expected to benefit. However, APBO #17 restricts the write-off period to a maximum of 40 years. Lewis calculated the amount of goodwill as $225,000. Exhibit 2, on page 121, explains that calculation.

Westford is curious about how Lewis determined the fair value for the printing equipment, which is the largest asset on the balance sheet. Lewis points out that APBO #16 provides general guidelines for assigning amounts to the individual assets acquired and liabilities assumed, except goodwill. APBO #16 requires that plant and equipment be valued either at the current replacement cost for similar capacity or at current net realizable value. Lewis explains that replacement cost is best represented by market values for similar assets. If market values are not readily available, then replacement cost can be estimated by either appraisal or a spe-

EXHIBIT 2
Calculation of Goodwill

Cost of investment in OLDCO		$5,000,000
Less: Net asset values		
Book values	$1,675,000	
Increases:		
Inventory	100,000	
Printing equipment (net)	3,000,000	
Fair values		4,775,000
Goodwill		$ 225,000

cific purchasing-power index. The net realizable value is determined by estimating the current selling price for the asset and subtracting disposal costs.

Lewis tells Westford that he obtained two separate estimates for the current market price to replace similar equipment. The estimates were very close and averaged out to $6 million. This is $3 million higher than the book value of the equipment. The $6 million is reflected on the worksheet used to prepare a postcombination balance sheet and appears in Exhibit 3 on page 122.

Westford expresses his concern about the future annual depreciation charges on the $6 million. Lewis informs him that the remaining useful life is estimated to be five years. Therefore, the annual depreciation charge will be $1,200,000. Westford states that this is twice the amount of prior years' depreciation. Westford asks Lewis what the depreciation charge would be if the equipment cost were estimated at net realizable value. Lewis explains that it is difficult to make relevant and reliable estimates of the net realizable value for assets such as property, plant, and equipment. Although he used net realizable value for the inventory, he believes that replacement cost is the appropriate valuation method for the LBO transaction under generally accepted accounting principles.

At this point, Westford becomes a bit weary of the accounting lesson. He asks Lewis whether he attempted to estimate the net realizable value. Lewis answers that he did obtain one estimate of $3,500,000 from a buyer in the secondhand market who expressed an interest in the equipment, assuming it is in good condition. Westford quickly calculates that the annual depreciation charge could be reduced by $500,000 if the equipment were recorded at the lower figure. Westford tells Lewis that the lower depreciation amount could make the difference between showing profits instead of losses over the next five years. According to Westford, this could be very important to NEWCO in securing needed funds in the future. Westford adds that he may decide to sell off the equipment soon after the purchase because of rapid change in printing technology. He concludes by stating: "I want you to record the equipment at $3,500,000."

EXHIBIT 3
Worksheet to Prepare a Postcombination Balance Sheet

	Borwood Acquisition ("NEWCO")	Borwood Printing ("OLDCO")	Adjustments	NEWCO (Post-combination)
Cash	1,000	100,000		101,000
Accounts receivable		300,000		300,000
Inventory		800,000	100,000	900,000
Printing equipment		6,000,000		6,000,000
Accumulated depreciation		(3,000,000)	3,000,000	0
Other equipment		200,000		200,000
Investment in OLDCO	5,000,000		(5,000,000)	0
Goodwill			225,000	225,000
Accounts payable		(700,000)		(700,000)
Accrued liabilities		(25,000)		(25,000)
Equipment notes payable to bank		(2,000,000)		(2,000,000)
Acquisition note payable to finance company	(5,000,000)			(5,000,000)
Stockholders' equity:				
Common stock:				
NEWCO	(1,000)			(1,000)
OLDCO		(100,000)	100,000	0
Retained earnings		(1,575,000)	1,575,000	0
	0	0	0	0

QUESTIONS

1. Discuss the theoretical justification for valuing the printing equipment at the current replacement cost as opposed to net realizable value in the LBO transaction. Would your answer be different if NEWCO were to sell off the old printing equipment soon after the purchase?
2. Assume you are in David Lewis's position. Evaluate the ethics of going along with Jim Westford's desire to record the equipment at net realizable value from a utilitarian and rights perspective.
3. If you were David Lewis, which provisions of the codes of conduct of the AICPA and IMA would be of greatest concern to you? What concerns would you have about your newly established employment relationship with Jim Westford and NEWCO?

Creative Toys, Inc.

∎

Sharon Browne is a certified public accountant (CPA) and a certified management accountant (CMA). She is also the controller and chief accounting officer of a large toy manufacturer, Creative Toys, Inc. The company has experienced a great deal of growth in sales since it went public in 1989. As controller, Browne is responsible for overseeing the work of the accounting department, which prepares financial statements for the company. Browne reports directly to the chief financial officer, Edie Wassler. Wassler is not a CPA or a CMA. Her background is in finance. Wassler reports directly to the chief executive officer, Sid Gurchick.

During the five years since the company went public, the sales revenue, profits, and earnings per share have all more than doubled. For the year ended December 31, 1994, the increases in these amounts were, respectively, 32, 57, and 40%. This growth was due, in large part, to the sales of a new product introduced during the holiday shopping season in November 1993. The product, "Chatter Chick," is a talking stuffed animal (chicken) that speaks prerecorded words and is able to move parts of its body. This product was extremely popular with prekindergarten children. Sales of the product were very strong through most of 1994. The income statement and balance sheet of Creative Toys, Inc., for 1993 and 1994 appear in Exhibit 1 on page 125.

While revenue from sales of Chatter Chicks had been increasing during the year since its introduction in November 1993, Sharon Browne was concerned that orders for future delivery of the product had declined in the latter half of 1994. This was the first decline in orders for the product since it was introduced in the market. The following is a summary of orders for the Chatter Chick during the quarters ended December 31, 1993, through December 31, 1994.

	12/31/93	**3/31/94**	**6/30/94**	**9/30/94**	**12/31/94**
Number of orders*	45,000	50,000	55,000	50,600	42,080
Incr. (Decr.) from					
prior quarter	—	11.1%	10.0%	(8.0%)	(16.8%)

*Orders indicated would be filled during the following quarter.

The company had built up a rather large inventory of Chatter Chicks during the latter half of 1994, anticipating continued growth in demand for the product throughout 1995. In fact, the December 31, 1994, total inventory for Creative Toys, Inc., was 85% above inventory levels at December 31, 1993. A large part of the inventory increase was attributable to finished Chatter Chick products. The company was also continuing to increase its purchases of raw materials for production of the product.

Browne was very concerned about the increasing inventory levels of the Chatter Chick, decreased demand for the product, and the effect of these factors on future salability and revenue for the company. Upon investigation, she learned from the marketing department that a competitor toy manufacturer had developed a more technologically advanced product than the Chatter Chick. This product, "Zoo Story," had the capability for narration of stories upon insertion of an audiotape in a compartment underneath one of a variety of animals that could be purchased. A reading book accompanied the tape so that a child could follow along in the book, looking at the pictures and words as the story about a favorite zoo animal unfolded. This product was an instant success upon entry into the toy market in August 1994.

Browne brought her concerns to the attention of Wassler during the course of the audit of the December 31, 1994, financial statements. Browne pointed out that during the first quarter of 1995, the company began to discount the price of Chatter Chicks in selling to department stores, in part because of the decreased demand and the competition from the Zoo Story products. The discount amounted to 30% of wholesale price. As a result, net realizable value was now 10% below the cost of the Chatter Chick. Browne recommended the establishment of at least a $500,000 inventory allowance at December 31, 1994. Browne's recommendation would have created a charge of approximately 10% against net income.

In February 1995, a meeting was scheduled of the audit committee and other members of the company's board of directors to discuss the December 31, 1994, financial statements. At this meeting, several members of the board pointedly questioned Gurchick about the decline in orders for Chatter Chick and the concurrent growth in inventory of this product. Two board members specifically asked Gurchick why an allowance had not been established. Gurchick pointed out that he had discussed this option with Wassler, based on a recommendation made by Browne. However, neither Gurchick nor Wassler could support the establishment of an allowance in the December 31, 1994, financial statements. They both felt that it would be premature at this date to write down the inventory for something that had not as yet happened. They pointed out that revenue, profits, and earnings per

EXHIBIT 1
Creative Toys, Inc.
Income Statement for the Years Ended
December 31, 1994 and 1993
(000 omitted)

	1994	1993
Revenue	$53,538	$40,560
Cost of sales	36,406	27,580
Gross margin	$17,132	$12,980
Operating expenses		
Research & development	$ 3,760	$ 2,900
Selling, general, & administrative	5,352	4,400
Total operating expenses	$ 9,112	$ 7,300
Operating profit	$ 8,020	$ 5,680
Other income	480	320
Profit before tax	$ 8,500	$ 6,000
Income tax	3,400	2,760
Net income	$ 5,100	$ 3,240
Earnings per share	$ 2.04	$ 1.62

Creative Toys, Inc.
Balance Sheet at December 31, 1994 and 1993
(000 omitted)

	1994	1993
Assets		
Cash	$ 1,096	$ 1,224
Marketable securities	338	412
Accounts receivable (net)	11,022	7,792
Inventories (at cost)	15,622	8,446
Prepaid expenses	312	386
Total current assets	$28,390	$18,260
Property, plant, & equipment (net)	8,944	6,822
Other	166	118
Total assets	$37,500	$25,200
Liabilities		
Accounts payable	$ 9,847	$ 4,562
Accrued liabilities	2,181	1,496
Total current liabilities	$12,028	$ 6,058
Long-term notes payable	5,822	4,422
Stockholders' Equity		
Common stock ($3 par)	7,500	6,000
Additional paid-in capital	7,875	6,300
Retained earnings	4,275	2,420
Total liabilities and stockholders' equity	$37,500	$25,200

share were at record levels for the company during the 12 months ended December 31, 1994. Although orders for future delivery of Chatter Chicks did decline during the latter half of the year, both Wassler and Gurchick believed that demand would pick up in 1995 because of the typically heavy sales volume during the summer months, when children are out of school. Gurchick informed the board that he was supported in this view by Stu Wise, the vice president of sales, who informed Gurchick that, during the months of July and August 1994, sales of the Chatter Chick were 20% higher than they had been for any other two-month period during that year.

Gurchick also pointed out that the company expected to make a public offering of stock in August of this year, in part to help finance production and distribution of a new product, "Wammer," which was scheduled to be in the department stores before the busy holiday shopping season. Gurchick believed this product would be very successful because it was patterned after the popular movie character of the same name. He felt that any significant reduction in profits and earnings per share, such as would be caused by the establishment of an inventory allowance, could negatively affect the company's ability to raise funds through the sale of stock. Gurchick also informed board members that he expected sales revenue from the Wammer product to more than offset any reduction in sales revenue from declining demand for the Chatter Chick. The anticipated sale of stock and related need to have attractive financial statements weighed quite heavily on the minds of many board members in accepting Gurchick's recommendation not to establish an inventory allowance at this time.

The situation did not improve during the first two quarters of 1995. In fact, total revenue had declined by 30%, when compared with the same period in 1994. Net income had declined by 33%. Approximately one-third of the decline in these amounts was attributable to the combined effect of a decline in price and reduction in quantity of product sold. Orders for the future delivery of the product were as follows:

	3/31/95	6/30/95
Number of orders	33,600	30,000
Incr. (Decr.) from prior quarter	(20.2%)	(10.7%)

Inventory levels were increasing because of continued high inventory levels of Chatter Chicks in anticipation of an increase in demand during the summer months. The ending inventory at June 30, 1995, was $18,746,000. This amount was 20% above inventory levels at December 31, 1994. One-third of this inventory value was the Chatter Chick product. This was of particular concern to Richard Newmann, the production manager, who contacted Gurchick in June and informed him that the Chatter Chick inventory was really stacking up. Newmann queried Gurchick about whether the company should begin to curtail production of this product. Gurchick told Newmann that he fully expected demand to increase during the summer months, so that inventory levels should soon begin to decline. Income statements for the first two quarters of 1995 are presented in Exhibit 2.

EXHIBIT 2
Creative Toys, Inc.
Quarterly Income Statements
(000 omitted)

	March 31, 1995	June 30, 1995
Revenue	$9,662	$9,118
Cost of sales	6,712	6,448
Gross margin	$2,950	$2,670
Operating expenses		
Research & development	$ 592	$ 520
Selling, general, & administrative	1,086	1,100
Total operating expenses	$1,678	$1,620
Operating profit	$1,272	$1,050
Other income	98	150
Profit before tax	$1,370	$1,200
Income tax	466	408
Net income	$ 904	$ 792
Earnings per share	$ .36	$ .32

Sales of Chatter Chicks were now very seriously and negatively affected by several competitor products, not just the Zoo Story product line. Prior to the public issuance of the June 30, 1995, quarterly report, Browne once again approached Wassler with her concerns. Browne strongly recommended the establishment of an inventory allowance for market decline in the June 30, 1995, quarterly report. Based on the fact that Chatter Chicks constituted one-third of ending inventory value at June 30, 1995, and the continuing 10% differential between the cost and net realizable value of the Chatter Chick, Browne recommended the establishment of an allowance of $625,000 as follows:

Inventory cost at June 30, 1995	$18,746,000
Percentage Chatter Chicks	× .3333
Chatter Chick value	$ 6,248,000
Differential	× .10
Allowance	$ 625,000

An allowance of this magnitude would reduce net income for the second quarter by $413,000 and earnings per share by $.17, or 52 and 53%, respectively. The new quarterly amount would be as follows (000 omitted):

	June 30, 1995
Reported profit before tax	$1,200
Less: Allowance	625
Profit before tax	$ 575
Income tax	196
Net income	$ 379
Earnings per share	$ .15

On a year-to-date basis, the proposed $625,000 allowance would reduce net income by 24% and earnings per share by 25%, determined as follows (000 omitted):

	March 31, 1995	June 30, 1995	Year-to-Date
Net income—reported	$904	$792	$1,696
Net income—proposed	904	379	1,283
Amount of decrease	—	$413	$ 413
Percentage reduction	—	52%	24%
Earnings per share—reported	$ .36	$ .32	$ .68
Earnings per share—proposed	.36	.15	.51
Amount of decrease	—	$ .17	$ .17
Percentage reduction	—	53%	25%

On July 15, 1995, prior to the issuance of the June 30, 1995, quarterly report, Sid Gurchick, Edie Wassler, and Sharon Browne met in order to discuss the status of Chatter Chick sales and the company's declining revenue, profits, and earnings per share. At this meeting, Browne reiterated her strong belief that a charge against income for the second quarter was appropriate because of the market decline in value of the Chatter Chick inventory. Although Gurchick and Wassler were sensitive to Browne's concerns, they could not support the establishment of an allowance at this time. Gurchick was still very concerned about the fact that the company expected to make a public offering of stock in August. He felt that any further reduction of profits and earnings per share in the second quarter would negatively affect the company's ability to raise funds through the sale of stock. Gurchick also informed Browne that he hoped the sales of the Wammer product during the last two months of the year would help the company to significantly increase its profitability for the year. If this was not the case, according to Gurchick, the company could reconsider an inventory write-down in the fourth quarter of the year.

Browne also pointed out to Gurchick that the internal auditors were questioning the absence of an inventory allowance. Additionally, Browne reminded Gurchick that the external auditors would be reviewing the quarterly data included in the annual report as part of their year-end audit work. Gurchick told Browne not to worry about the internal auditors. He would take care of their concerns. As to the external auditors, Gurchick told Browne that, since he expected to see significant improvement in revenue and profitability by year-end, it would be more acceptable to establish a charge against income under those conditions, should the auditors insist on doing this. Additionally, Wassler reminded Browne that the auditors' review of the quarterly information was retrospective. That is, it occurred after the close, with the year-end audit work, rather than prior to public release of quarterly information. Both Gurchick and Wassler felt that, under these circumstances, it was unlikely the auditors would question the company's failure to establish an allowance for inventory market decline in the quarterly reports.

The meeting abruptly came to an end when Browne restated her strong belief that the inventory should be written down in the June 30, 1995, quarterly report. Gurchick then reminded Browne that bonuses to top corporate officials were based, in part, on quarterly profits, and an inventory write-down of the magnitude she was suggesting would negatively affect the welfare of many top corporate officials, including herself, as well as the employees and stockholders of the company. Gurchick strongly suggested that Browne reconsider her position on this issue. At this point, Browne went back to her office to consider her options.

QUESTIONS

1. An important issue raised by the facts of this case is the usefulness of quarterly information to users of quarterly financial reports. How does this issue relate to Sid Gurchick's position that inventory could be written down in the fourth quarter of the year, rather than earlier in the year, if demand for the Chatter Chick product did not improve by year-end?
2. What do you think about the corporate culture at Creative Toys?
3. Assume that Sharon Browne is a member of the American Institute of Certified Public Accountants and the Institute of Management Accountants. What alternative courses of action exist for her? Now, assume you are in her position. What would you do? Discuss the possible implications of any action(s) you decide to take.

United Thermostatic Controls

■

United Thermostatic Controls is engaged in the manufacturing and marketing of residential and commercial thermostats. The thermostats are used to regulate temperature in furnaces and refrigerators. United sells its product primarily to retailers in the domestic market. The company is headquartered in San Jose, California. Its operations are decentralized according to geographic region. United is a publicly owned company, and its common stock is listed and traded on the New York Stock Exchange. The organization chart for United is presented in Figure 1 on page 131.

Frank Campbell is the director of the Southern sales division. Worsening regional economic conditions and a reduced rate of demand for United's products together have created pressures to nonetheless achieve sales revenue targets set by United management. Also, significant pressures exist within the organization for sales divisions to maximize their revenues and earnings for 1994 in anticipation of a public offering of stock early in 1995. Budgeted and actual sales revenue amounts, by division, for the first three quarters in 1994 are presented in Exhibit 1 on page 132.

Campbell knows that actual sales lagged even further behind budgeted sales during the first two months of the fourth quarter. He also knows that each of the other three sales divisions exceeded their budgeted sales amounts during the first three quarters in 1994. He is very concerned that the Southern division has been unable to meet or exceed budgeted sales amounts. He is particularly worried about the effect this might have on his and the division managers' bonuses and share of corporate profits.

In an attempt to improve the sales revenue of the Southern division for the fourth quarter and for the year ended December 31, 1994, Campbell reviewed purchase orders received during the latter half of November and early December in order to determine whether shipments could be made to customers prior to December 31.

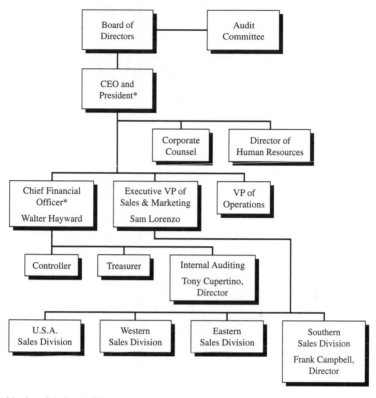

FIGURE 1
Organization Chart

Campbell knows that sometimes orders that are received before year-end can be filled by December 31, thereby enabling the division to record the sales revenue during the current fiscal year. It could simply be a matter of accelerating production and shipping in order to increase sales revenue for the year.

Reported sales revenue of the Southern division for the fourth quarter of 1994 was $792,000. This represented a 18.6% increase over the actual sales revenue for the third quarter of the year. As a result of this increase, reported sales revenue for the fourth quarter exceeded the budgeted amount by $80,000, or 11.2%. Actual sales revenue for the year exceeded the budgeted amount for the Southern division by $14,000, or .5%. Budgeted and actual sales revenue amounts, by division, for the year ended December 31, 1994, are presented in Exhibit 2 on page 132.

During the course of their test of controls, the internal audit staff questioned the appropriateness of recording revenue of $150,000 on two shipments made by the

EXHIBIT 1
United Thermostatic Controls
Budgeted and Actual Sales Revenue
First Three Quarters in 1994

Quarter Ended	U.S.A. Sales Division			Western Sales Division			Eastern Sales Division			Southern Sales Division		
	Budget	Actual	% Var.	Budget	Actual	% Var.	Budget	Actual	% Var.	Budget	Actual	% Var.
March 31	$ 632,000	$ 638,000	.009	$ 886,000	$ 898,000	.014	$ 743,000	$ 750,000	.009	$ 688,000	$ 680,000	(.012)
June 30	640,000	642,000	.003	908,000	918,000	.011	752,000	760,000	.011	696,000	674,000	(.032)
September 30	648,000	656,000	.012	930,000	936,000	.006	761,000	769,000	.011	704,000	668,000	(.051)
Through September 30	$1,920,000	$1,936,000	.008	$2,724,000	$2,752,000	.010	$2,256,000	$2,279,000	.010	$2,088,000	$2,022,000	(.032)

EXHIBIT 2
United Thermostatic Controls
Budgeted and Actual Sales Revenue
For the Year Ended December 31, 1994

Quarter Ended	U.S.A. Sales Division			Western Sales Division			Eastern Sales Division			Southern Sales Division		
	Budget	Actual	% Var.	Budget	Actual	% Var.	Budget	Actual	% Var.	Budget	Actual	% Var.
March 31	$ 632,000	$ 638,000	.009	$ 886,000	$ 898,000	.014	$ 743,000	$ 750,000	.009	$ 688,000	$ 680,000	(.012)
June 30	640,000	642,000	.003	908,000	918,000	.011	752,000	760,000	.011	696,000	674,000	(.032)
September 30	648,000	656,000	.012	930,000	936,000	.006	761,000	769,000	.011	704,000	668,000	(.051)
December 31	656,000	662,000	.009	952,000	958,000	.006	770,000	778,000	.010	712,000	792,000	.112
1994 Totals	$2,576,000	$2,598,000	.009	$3,676,000	$3,710,000	.009	$3,026,000	$3,057,000	.010	$2,800,000	$2,814,000	.005

133

Southern division in the fourth quarter of the year. These shipments are described below.

1. United shipped thermostats to Allen Corporation on December 31, 1994, and billed Allen $85,000, even though Allen had specified an earliest delivery date of February 1, 1995. Allen intended to use the thermostats in the heating system of a new building that would not be ready for occupancy until March 1, 1995.
2. United shipped thermostats to Bilco Corporation on December 30, 1994, in partial fulfillment of an order. United recorded $65,000 revenue on that date. Bilco had previously specified that partial shipments would not be accepted. Delivery of the full shipment had been scheduled for February 1, 1995.

During their investigation, the internal auditors learned that Campbell had placed pressure on the accountants to record these two shipments early in order to enable the Southern division to achieve its goals regarding the company's revenue targets. The auditors were concerned about the appropriateness of recording the $150,000 revenue in 1994 in the absence of an expressed or implied agreement with the customers to accept and pay for the prematurely shipped merchandise. The auditors noted that, had the revenue from these two shipments not been recorded, the Southern division's actual sales for the fourth quarter would have been below the budgeted amount by $70,000, or 9.8%. Actual sales revenue for the year ended December 31, 1994, would have been below the budgeted amount by $136,000, or 4.9%. The revenue effect of the two shipments in question created a 5.4% shift in the variance between actual and budgeted sales for the year. The auditors felt that this effect was significant with respect to the division's revenue and earnings for the fourth quarter and for the year ended December 31, 1994. The auditors decided to take their concerns to Tony Cupertino, the director of the internal auditing department.

Cupertino discussed the situation with Campbell. Campbell informed Cupertino that he had received assurances from Sam Lorenzo, executive vice president of sales and marketing, that top management would support the recording of the $150,000 revenue because of its strong desire to meet or exceed budgeted revenue and earnings amounts. In fact, Lorenzo had stated to Campbell that he did not see anything wrong with recording the revenue in 1994, since the merchandise had been shipped to the customers before year-end and the terms of shipment were FOB shipping point.

At this point, Cupertino is uncertain whether he should take his concerns to Walter Hayward, the chief financial officer, who is also a member of the board of directors, or take them directly to the audit committee. Cupertino is not even certain that he should pursue the matter any further, because of the financial performance pressures that exist within the organization. However, he is very concerned about his responsibility to coordinate the work of the internal auditing department with that of the external auditors.

QUESTION

Assume that Tony Cupertino is a CPA and a member of the American Institute of Certified Public Accountants. He is also a CIA and a member of the Institute of Internal Auditors. Use the seven-step ethical decision-making process and reason out what action Cupertino should take in this situation.

Milton Manufacturing Company

■

Milton Manufacturing Company produces a variety of textiles for distribution to wholesale manufacturers of clothing products. Milton's primary operations are located in Long Island City, New York, with branch factories and warehouses in more than a dozen other cities.

Milton's stock is listed on the over-the-counter exchange. It sold $1,200,000 of common stock during the past two years in order to finance its growing operations. Because these issuances did not provide enough funds for the company's continued operations, Milton planned to float a $5-million bond issue during the first quarter of 1995.

The president of Milton Manufacturing is Alan Bush. Early in 1994, Bush met with the controller, Lynn Carnes, to discuss ways in which Milton could better control cash outflows during 1994. They were concerned because the planned bond sale could be hampered by the net cash outflows that occurred during the past two years. The cash flow statements of Milton Manufacturing Company for 1992 and 1993 appear in Exhibit 1 on page 137.

It was decided at the meeting that capital expenditures had to be better controlled. There was a 26% increase in these expenditures during 1993. Both Bush and Carnes were concerned that an increase of similar proportions in 1994 could negatively affect Milton's ability to successfully float its $5-million bond issue. Therefore, a policy was established that each plant's capital expenditures could not exceed the amount incurred in 1992.

Stuart West is the plant manager at the Long Island City location. West was informed of the new capital expenditure policy by Howard Hurst, the vice president for operations. West told Hurst that the new policy could negatively affect plant operations because certain machinery, essential to the production process, had been breaking down more frequently during the past two years. The problem was

EXHIBIT 1
Milton Manufacturing Company
Statement of Cash Flows
For the Years Ended
December 31, 1993 and 1992
(000 omitted)

	December 31, 1993	December 31, 1992
Cash Flows from Operating Activities:		
Net income	$ 372	$ 542
Adjustments to reconcile net income to net cash provided by operating activities:		
Depreciation, amortization, and retirements .	1,209	1,030
Decrease (increase) in receivables	60	(37)
Decrease (increase) in inventories	38	9
Increase (decrease) in payables and accrued liabilities	(183)	79
Deferred taxes	226	302
Net cash provided by operating activities	$ 1,722	$ 1,925
Cash Flows from Investing Activities:		
Capital expenditures	$(2,420)	$(1,918)
Proceeds from dispositions of property	150	90
Investments in stocks and bonds	(96)	(22)
Proceeds from sales of investments	122	16
Net cash used in investing activities	$(2,244)	$(1,834)
Cash Flows from Financing Activities:		
Repayment of long-term debt	$ —	$ (570)
Cash dividends paid	(452)	(386)
Issuances of common stock	620	580
Net cash provided by (used in) financing activities	$ 168	$ (376)
Increase (decrease) in cash and cash equivalents	$ (354)	$ (285)
Cash and cash equivalents— beginning of year	506	791
Cash and cash equivalents— end of year	$ 152	$ 506

primarily with the motors. New and better models with more efficient motors had been developed by an overseas supplier. These were expected to be available in mid-1994. West planned to order 100 of these new machines for the Long Island City operation, and he expected that other plant managers would do the same. Hurst suggested that any such acquisition be delayed about one year so that Milton first completes its bond issuance. It was likely that the restrictions on capital expenditures would be lifted after the bonds were issued. In any case, the cost of the new machines for all plant locations would clearly exceed allowed expenditure levels. Also, the plant was already committed to other capital expenditures for 1994. West reluctantly agreed to Hurst's suggestion.

Milton Manufacturing operated very profitably during the first six months of 1994. Net cash inflows from all activities exceeded outflows by $96,000 during this time period. Both Bush and Carnes were very satisfied with these results. They felt quite confident that if the second half of the year was as successful as the first half, then Milton would have no trouble raising needed funds through the planned bond issuance.

Production activities accelerated during the third quarter as a result of increased demand for Milton's textiles. This put additional pressure on those machines that already had been breaking down more frequently. West and the other plant managers were concerned about this because their primary responsibility was to ensure that the production process operated smoothly. The last thing anyone needed right now was a stoppage of production because of machine failure. It was at this time that disturbing information came to West's attention. The plant's primary supplier of motors for the production machinery announced a 25% price increase effective January 2, 1995. This supplier had been charging about 25% less than other suppliers. West knew that there would be no alternative in the future but to acquire the motors at a significantly higher cost.

After careful consideration, West suggested to the other plant managers that they accelerate ordering the motors to a date before the price increase takes effect on January 2, 1995. He was convinced that this was the proper action to take, despite the capital expenditure policy. It was essential to have an adequate supply of replacement parts for the machinery to ensure continued efficient production operations. During the last few months of 1994, the Long Island City plant alone ordered $150,000 of replacement parts. These were charged to expenses.

Profitable operations continued for Milton Manufacturing through the latter half of 1994. The company ended the year with net income reported as $428,000, a 15% increase over 1993. Net cash inflows from cash and cash equivalent activities exceeded outflows by $140,000, a 140% increase over 1993. The cash flow statement of Milton Manufacturing Company for 1994 appears in Exhibit 2 on page 139.

The internal auditors were reviewing the accounting procedures at the Long Island City plant shortly after the close of the year ended December 31, 1994. While investigating inventory practices, one of the auditors noticed that there was a huge supply of motors in the production area. There appeared to be hundreds of these motors. A complete inventory was taken. It was determined that there were 1,000 motors stored in the production area. This was brought to the attention of Edith Braun, the chief internal auditor. She contacted Carnes to inquire whether the latter was aware that a significant amount of replacement parts had been acquired and were being stored in the production area. Carnes stated that she had not been informed of this.

EXHIBIT 2
Milton Manufacturing Company
Statement of Cash Flows
For the Year Ended December 31, 1994
(000 omitted)

Cash Flows from Operating Activities:

Net income	$ 428
Adjustments to reconcile net income to net	
cash provided by operating activities:	
Depreciation, amortization, and retirements	1,418
Decrease (increase) in receivables	122
Decrease (increase) in inventories	44
Increase (decrease) in payables and accrued liabilities	66
Deferred taxes	244
Net cash provided by operating activities	$ 2,322

Cash Flows from Investing Activities:

Capital expenditures	$(1,908)
Proceeds from dispositions of property	210
Investments in stocks and bonds	(44)
Proceeds from sales of investments	102
Net cash used in investing activities	$(1,640)

Cash Flows from Financing Activities:

Cash dividends paid	$ (542)
Net cash provided by (used in) financing activities	$ (542)
Increase (decrease) in cash and cash equivalents	$ 140
Cash and cash equivalents—beginning of year	152
Cash and cash equivalents—end of year	$ 292

Braun and Carnes contacted Hurst, who expressed surprise about the amount of replacement parts that had been acquired. It was determined that almost a two-year supply existed at the Long Island City plant. A complete inventory at all plants revealed that $400,000 of replacement parts had been charged to expenses during the last few months of 1994. The two requested a meeting with West. During the meeting West explained the reasons for building up a large supply of motors.

Braun and Carnes pointedly questioned West about the propriety of his actions. West insisted that he had saved Milton Manufacturing $100,000 by acquiring the parts prior to the supplier's planned price increase. West felt that he exercised good judgment under the circumstances. He reminded Braun and Carnes of his primary responsibility to keep the plant operating as efficiently as possible. Furthermore, West felt that his options were limited by company policy, since he could not acquire the more efficient machinery that had become available in mid-1994.

Braun and Carnes expressed sensitivity to West's situation. However, they were very concerned about the effect of his actions and those of the other plant managers on the integrity of the accounting and financial reporting process.

QUESTIONS

1. Evaluate Stuart West's actions and their related effects on the current and future operations of Milton Manufacturing Company from an ethical reasoning perspective.
2. What ethical and professional concerns exist for Edith Braun and Lynn Carnes in deciding upon a course of action? What should Braun and Carnes do?

Pirate Steel Company

∎

Pirate Steel Company is a large processor of steel products that are manufactured in the United States and sold to customers in the United States and in several other countries. Pirate Steel is considered to be a leader in the steel industry and has operated profitably for many years. However, during the 1980s, increased foreign competition threatened to significantly affect the profitability of the company.

Pirate Steel had never been too cost-conscious in its production operations, because it was always able to meet or exceed targeted profit margins. Whenever raw material or other production costs increased, Pirate Steel would increase its selling price accordingly. As a result of increased competition, however, the company began to focus more attention on cost control. It did not want to lose its competitive position in the marketplace.

Bill Stargol is the vice president for production of Pirate Steel. He just completed a meeting with the top management at which he was informed that, effective immediately, a full-scale effort would be made to control all costs in order to maintain profit margins. Top management was specifically concerned about the large amounts of repair and maintenance costs that were incurred each year. Stargol was told that the new policy was necessary because of decreased price flexibility as a result of increased foreign competition.

According to the new cost control policy, every effort must be made in order to defer discretionary repairs and maintenance to machinery and equipment. Each request for such expenditure had to be personally approved by the foreperson on the job, the production manager (Dick Grote), and Stargol. The burden of proof was clearly placed on the production people, who had to justify repair and maintenance expenditures.

The production staff greeted the new policy with a great deal of resistance. Grote pointed out that the potential existed for machine breakdowns that could cost Pirate Steel more money in the long run than would be spent if needed repairs were made on a timely basis. He also reminded Stargol that preventive maintenance was a critical component of efficient operations.

No one in the production department was very happy about the new controls on repair and maintenance expenditures. Everyone, from top management down to the forepeople on the various jobs, knew that they had to do everything possible to keep the operation running. They suspected that they would be blamed if the equipment failed causing delays in jobs, even though the new cost control policy made it more difficult to make the needed repairs. Machine breakdowns would lead to further downward pressure on profit margins, which could lead to cost cutbacks, employee layoffs, and even discontinuance of marginal operations.

As a result of the pressure to control costs, a somewhat devious strategy developed among the forepersons. Specifically, in order to have a repair and maintenance request approved, the job foreperson had to write up the work order in such a way that it sounded as though significant improvements to the equipment would result from the proposed expenditure. It was not enough to simply state that something was broken and you wanted to fix it. Instead, a strong case had to be made that the equipment would operate much more efficiently as a result of the expenditure and, in the long run, cost savings would result. In other words, the job forepeople had to overstate their case to such an extent that Grote and Stargol would have no choice but to approve the expenditure.

Over $100 million was charged to repairs and maintenance during a 12-month period ending on December 31, 1993. At the conclusion of the year, management somewhat relaxed its restrictive policies toward repair and maintenance costs because of improvements in the competitive position of Pirate Steel. However, work orders continued to be consistently overstated so that the requests would be approved. This practice continued into 1994.

Elroy Faze is a CPA and a CMA. He is the controller of Pirate Steel. Faze was aware of the company's repair and maintenance policy. He did not know, however, that work-order requests were being processed based on false and misleading information about the benefits of proposed repair and maintenance expenditures. This fact came to his attention as a result of the internal auditor's annual review of internal accounting controls, including the accounting system for authorizing and recording repair and maintenance transactions.

Faze realized that the $100 million amount had a potential significant effect on the profitability of Pirate Steel for the year ended December 31, 1993. He was concerned that the external auditors would question the accounting for repair and maintenance expenditures because of the descriptions included in the work orders. Many of the descriptions made it sound as though a new piece of equipment resulted from the expenditures. Ironically, all such expenditures were properly expensed, even though the descriptions made it sound as though the items should have been capitalized. The reason is that the standard repair and maintenance request forms were used to process the expenditures that were approved by Grote and Stargol.

Elroy Faze requested a meeting with Stargol and Sid Thryft, chief executive officer of Pirate Steel. Faze expressed his concerns about the treatment of repair and maintenance expenditures and the supporting descriptions in the work orders. According to Faze, the external auditors might question the treatment of these expenditures based on the descriptions. The Internal Revenue Service might question them, as well, and, possibly, disallow deductions for these items. Such action would significantly affect Pirate Steel's tax obligation for 1993 and for subsequent years. Agreement was reached to end the cost-control policy, so that any potential effects would be limited to 1993.

Thryft understood Faze's concerns but did not appear to be worried about any potential audit or tax adjustments. He told Faze: "If the auditors or the IRS question the descriptions and expense treatment, then we will explain the reasons for that treatment to them."

Faze understood Thryft's point of view on this matter. However, he was concerned with more than just potential audit and/or tax adjustments. He was also very concerned about the repair and maintenance policy and its effect on the operations of the production department and the integrity of its personnel. He went on to explain that the policy was producing undesirable short-term behavioral effects that could have long-term negative implications for Pirate Steel. It was his belief that the policy was "forcing" the operating people to fictionalize in writing up the work orders. He was concerned that a culture was developing whereby employees felt justified in "slanting" information to achieve a desired goal. Faze suggested that the policy was fostering dishonesty and noted that he was greatly concerned about the resulting corporate climate. He recommended that Pirate Steel initiate a major education campaign to explain to its employees how to write a work order.

Faze concluded by suggesting that the matter be brought to the attention of the audit committee. Thryft cautioned Faze against this and stated: "Why create problems for the company when none exist? The 1993 financial statements were correct. The inaccurate descriptions reflected an internal problem that has no bearing on auditors' responsibilities. Therefore, I see no reason to involve the audit committee. Moreover, there have been no violations of the company's code of ethics."

QUESTIONS

1. Sid Thryft stated in the concluding sentence that there have been no violations of the corporate code of ethics. How does compliance with a code of ethics relate to virtue, and what is ethical from a rights or justice point of view? What do you think about the company's cost-control policy from both an operational and an ethical perspective?

2. Discuss the ethical and professional responsibilities of Elroy Faze in this situation. What would you do if you were in his position? Discuss the possible implications of any action(s) you might decide to take.

Larkin Petroleum Company

■

Larkin Petroleum Company produces and distributes oil, liquefied petroleum gas, and natural gas. These products consist of highly flammable hydrocarbons and are used primarily as fuel or as raw material for chemical synthesis. Larkin serves a broad range of industrial users in a very competitive environment.

Larkin operates a separate division for each of its product lines. Each division is treated almost as an independent enterprise, with its own accounting and operations management functions. The internal auditing function is decentralized so that each division has its own auditors. The director of internal auditing reports directly to the divisional vice president. Centralized management consists of human resources, legal services, corporate auditing, corporate accounting, and financial management functions. The chief executive officer of Larkin Petroleum is Jack Harper. Harper reports to the board of directors and the audit committee.

NATURAL GAS DIVISION

Cliff Byrnes is the vice president of the natural gas division. Reporting directly to Byrnes are the controller, Harvey Smithfeld; the director of internal auditing, Martin Stone; and the directors of production and of sales, respectively, Peter Anderson and George Lee. A partial organization chart for the natural gas division is presented in Figure 1 on page 145.

Production Environment

The accounting department is responsible for maintaining proper accounting records, including product cost records. Bob Weston is the manager of the department. He reports directly to Smithfeld. One member of the accounting staff,

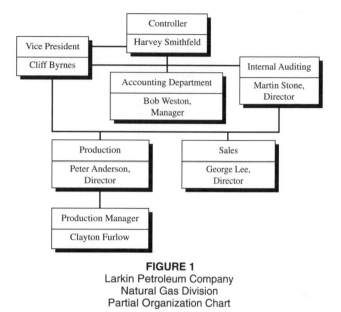

FIGURE 1
Larkin Petroleum Company
Natural Gas Division
Partial Organization Chart

James Bowmont, works directly with the production staff and he is responsible for calculating product yields.

Clayton Furlow is the production manager. He reports directly to Anderson. Furlow's responsibilities include inventory record keeping. He has a staff of three people, all of whom assist in the record-keeping function.

At Larkin Petroleum, product yields are used to evaluate the success of the production process. Yields are also used to determine annual bonus payments to production managers. Typically, yield amounts fluctuate over a period of time, reflecting varying levels of production efficiency and any problems with the production process.

During a routine investigation of inventory by the internal auditing staff, it was determined that yields were being consistently overstated. For example, during the recent three-year period, yield amounts were recorded each year at around 100%. The internal auditors noted that during this period of time inventory losses were also being recorded. Upon further investigation, the auditors discovered a flaw in the production process. A significant amount of product was actually lost as a result of the defect. It had been more difficult to identify the process failure during the three-year period because of the consistent overstatement of yields.

Internal Audit Investigation

The internal auditors conducted an exhaustive investigation after uncovering the overstated yields. They determined that yield amounts had been calculated by the production staff rather than by the accounting department. These amounts were given to Bowmont, who recorded them without independent calculation or verification. It was determined that Furlow was responsible for overstating the yields. Furlow acted in complicity with the production staff. As a result of the overstated yields, Furlow had received bonus payments in excess of the amount that he was entitled to receive.

The overstated yields had two significant consequences for Larkin Petroleum, as follows:

1. Excessive Product Costs. Excessive product costs resulted from the increased use of ingredients in the production process. This was not discovered earlier because the overstated yields masked the problem with the production process. Corporate and divisional profits were lower than they should have been. Had the flaw been discovered sooner, it could have been corrected at a nominal cost in comparison with the additional product costs that were now being incurred.

2. Excessive Compensation Payments. Furlow's compensation was higher than it should have been. He received an excessive amount in bonuses, since the bonus payments were based on the 100% reported yield amounts. The excessive payments to Furlow did not affect Larkin's total profits. However, they did result in an unfair distribution of the total corporate bonus pool; that is, other managers did not receive their fair share.

The internal auditors gathered together all of the necessary documentation to support their charge of overstated yields and met with Stone. Stone reviewed the documentation, and he came to the same conclusion that his internal auditing staff had reached. However, he was not sure what to do at this point—in part, because of the professional and personal relationship that he had with Furlow. Stone knew that Furlow was well respected within the organization. They had a good working relationship, and Stone considered Furlow to be a good friend.

Stone decided to set up a meeting with Furlow. When confronted with the irrefutable evidence provided by Stone, Furlow admitted that he did overstate the production yields. Furlow pointed out to Stone that he "never did anything like this before." In fact, Furlow's record at Larkin Petroleum was an exemplary one during the 18 years that he had worked for the company. Furlow offered his complete cooperation in order to correct the flaw in the production process. He did, however, appeal to Stone not to pursue the matter any further.

QUESTIONS

1. Discuss the implications of the organizational structure of Larkin Petroleum Company with respect to the independence of its internal auditing function.
2. Discuss how Martin Stone's actions might affect the fair distribution of the company's resources to its stakeholders.
3. Assume you are in Stone's position. To whom do you owe loyalty in making a decision whether to pursue the matter any further within the organization. If Stone is a CPA and CIA, what steps should he take in this matter?

CASES

INTERNATIONAL ENVIRONMENT

Ethics in the International Environment

■

BACKGROUND

Perhaps the most difficult decision for the management of a multinational enterprise to make concerns whether to adhere to host-country standards and customs when operating abroad or to conduct global operations in accordance with the home country's own ethical standards, laws, and customs, instead. The issue of whether to act in accordance with one's own standards or the local customs can create ethical dilemmas for a multinational manager. For example, a U.S. manager might be offered a gift by the manager of a Japanese supplier. That gift could be interpreted as a friendly gesture, an expression of gratitude, or a bribe—depending upon the cultural context and how the receiver interprets the intention of the giver of the gift. In Japan, the giving of gifts is considered to be an important part of building a relationship with another person. The Japanese culture emphasizes the individual's role as a member of a group or the family unit. Gift giving can be an important step toward acceptance and becoming a member of the group. The U.S. culture, on the other hand, emphasizes individual action and responsibility, so the gift could be interpreted as an attempt to influence the decisions of the U.S. manager.

Ethical standards differ around the world, in part, because of cultural influences. The culture of a country reflects the ideas, habits, attitudes, customs, and traditions of that society. These factors influence the accepted ways of doing business in a particular society. Culture acts as a filter to influence the perceptions of events. For example, culture influences the degree of acceptance of certain payments that are made to influence the actions of those in authority.

FOREIGN CORRUPT PRACTICES ACT

The Foreign Corrupt Practices Act of 1977 (FCPA) establishes standards for the acceptability of payments made by U.S. multinationals or their agents to foreign government officials. Bartley Brennan analyzes the business community's reactions to the FCPA and to subsequent amendments to the act in 1988. According to Brennan, the antibribery provisions were criticized by many businesses as creating a negative impact on the ability of U.S. corporations to compete abroad and for the lack of clarity in some of the provisions of the act. He cites a 1981 report of the General Accounting Office that presents the results of a survey of U.S. corporations. The data indicate that 30% of the corporations lost business overseas as a result of the act and 70% rated the clarity of at least one of the antibribery provisions as "inadequate" or "very inadequate." The major ambiguities noted by the respondents include (1) whether a payment is a bribe (illegal under FCPA) or a "facilitating payment" (legal payment), (2) the degree of responsibility a company has for the actions of its foreign agents, and (3) the definition of the term *foreign official*.[1]

A summary of the antibribery provisions of the FCPA and related amendments that were passed in 1988 appears in Exhibit 1 on page 151.

Facilitating Payments versus Bribes

An important distinction in evaluating the ethical propriety of payments made to third parties is whether such payments are "grease" (or "facilitating payments"), which are permitted under the amended act, or whether they are "bribes," which are not permitted. Facilitating payments are small amounts paid to clerks or officials in hopes of persuading them to perform their normal duties faster or better. These payments do not alter the decisions of third parties; instead, they seek to secure what already is part of the responsibilities of the third party. For example, a $50 payment to a customs official to allow a U.S. multinational to bring a permitted item into the foreign country would constitute a grease payment.

A *bribe* is a payment made to someone in order to secure a sale or in order to obtain approval or assistance from that individual or organization. Although they are accepted commercial transactions in some parts of the world, in the United States we view these payments as ethically improper. Even in those areas where such payments are an acceptable custom in business transactions, bribery tends to be against the local law. Moreover, the public is usually outraged when bribery is disclosed. This was the case in the United States in 1977 when the Securities and Exchange Commission (SEC) cited 527 companies for bribes and other dubious payments that were made in order to win foreign contracts between 1960 and 1977. The payments came to light through its voluntary disclosure plan. Lockheed Corporation was one of the companies caught in the scandal. It was determined that Lockheed had made about $55 million in illegal payments to foreign govern-

---

[1]Brennan, Bartley A., "The Foreign Corrupt Practices Act Amendments of 1988: 'Death' of a Law," *North Carolina Journal of International Law & Commerce Regulation,* volume 15 (1990), pp. 229–247.

EXHIBIT 1
Antibribery Provisions of the 1977 Foreign
Corrupt Practices Act and 1988 Amendments

Foreign Corrupt Practices Act of 1977

On December 20, 1977, President Carter signed into law the Foreign Corrupt Practices Act (FCPA) following the voluntary disclosure of more than $300 million in payments to foreign governments and political parties. The act makes it a crime to offer or provide payments to officials of foreign governments, political candidates, or political parties for the purpose of obtaining or retaining business. It applies to all U.S. corporations, whether they are publicly or privately held, and to foreign companies filing with the SEC.

Under the 1977 act, a corporation that violates the law can be fined up to $1 million, while its officers who directly participated in violations of the act or had "reason to know" of such violations can be fined up to $10,000 and/or imprisoned for up to five years. The act also prohibits corporations from indemnifying fines imposed on their directors, officers, employees, or agents. The act does not prohibit grease payments to foreign government employees whose duties are primarily ministerial or clerical, since such payments are sometimes required in order to persuade recipients to perform their normal duties.*

1988 Amendments

As a result of the criticisms of the antibribery provisions of the 1977 FCPA, Congress amended the act in 1988 to clarify the definition of *prohibited payments.* On August 23, 1988, President Reagan signed into law the amendments as part of an overall bill, the Omnibus Trade and Competitiveness Act of 1988.†

The major changes to the 1977 FCPA are as follows:

- A payment is defined as illegal if it is intended to influence a foreign official to act in a way that is incompatible with the official's legal duty.
- The "reason to know" standard is replaced by a "knowing" standard, so that criminal liability for illegal payments to third parties applies to individuals who "knowingly" engage in or tolerate illegal payments under the act.
- The definition of permissible facilitating, or "grease" payments, is expanded to include payments to any foreign official if they are facilitating or expediting payments for the purpose of expediting or securing the performance of a routine governmental action.

Examples: (1) Obtaining permits, licenses, or the official documents to qualify a person to do business in a foreign country; (2) processing governmental papers, such as visas and work orders; (3) providing police protection, mail pickup and delivery, or scheduling inspections associated with contract performance or inspections related to the transit of goods across country; (4) providing telephone service, providing power and water, loading and unloading cargo, or protecting perishable products or commodities from deterioration; and (5) actions of a similar nature.

---

*15 U.S.C. Section 78 dd (1982). (continued)
†15 U.S.C. Section 78 dd (1988).

EXHIBIT 1 *(continued)*
Antibribery Provisions of the 1977 Foreign
Corrupt Practices Act and 1988 Amendments

- Two affirmative defenses are provided for those accused of violating the FCPA, as follows: (1) The payment can be made to a foreign official if it is lawful "under the written laws" of the foreign country and (2) the payment can be made for "reasonable and bona fide expenditures."

Examples: Travel and lodging expenses incurred by or for a foreign official, party, party official, or candidate that are "directly related to": (a) the promotion, demonstration, or explanation of products or services; or (b) the execution or performance of a contract with a foreign government or agency thereof.

- Individuals can be prosecuted for violations even if the firm for which they work is not guilty. (The 1977 act prevented the prosecution of employees or agents unless the entity itself was found to have violated the FCPA.)
- Penalties for violations are raised to $2 million for firms and $100,000 for individuals. Imprisonment is retained at five years. A new $10,000 civil penalty is enacted.

---

ments and officials. One such payment of $1.7 million to Japanese Premier Tanaka led to his resignation in disgrace in 1974.[2]

Accounting Considerations and the FCPA

The accounting issues related to the FCPA focus on the adequacy of internal controls. The law requires SEC registrants to maintain internal accounting controls in order to ensure that all transactions are authorized by management and recorded properly. Of course, this is nothing new for the accounting profession. Statement on Auditing Standards No. 1 clarifies that it is management's responsibility to adopt sound accounting policies and to establish and maintain an internal control structure adequate to record, process, summarize, and report financial data that are consistent with management's assertions in the financial statements. Management can address its responsibilities in this regard in its report entitled *Management's Responsibility for Financial Reporting.* This report is included in the annual reports of many public companies.

The position of the accounting profession is that the entity's compliance with the FCPA is a legal determination. According to Statement on Standards for Attestation Engagements (SSAE) No. 2, accountants may be engaged to provide an opinion on management's assertions about the effectiveness of an entity's internal

---

[2]Ramsey, Richard D., and A. F. Alkhafaji, "The 1977 Foreign Corrupt Practices Act and the 1988 Omnibus Trade Bill," *Management Decision,* volume 29, no. 6.

control structure. However, the accountants' report should not indicate whether an entity is in compliance with the provisions of the FCPA.

Ethical Considerations and the FCPA

There are many ethical issues that can be raised about the propriety of bribery. One point of view is that we have no right to impose our values on others. However, the fact is, we already do this when legal rights exist. For example, making or distributing unauthorized copies of copyrighted material violates U.S. copyright law. The Software Publishers Association and the Business Software Alliance estimated that 1993 worldwide losses from pirated software were between $7.4 billion and $12.8 billion. The United States has made piracy a major issue in its relations with some Asian countries that view copyrighted software as something that should be shared with all for the benefit of society. Our government emphasizes the importance of the rights of the individual who created the software and supports the concept of intellectual property rights as it exists in international law.

Some in business view bribe payments as a necessary cost of doing business in certain countries. However, from an ethical perspective, a bribe payment gives an unfair advantage to the paying party. Moreover, if everyone bribed officials in order to secure business—then the manner in which products are sold would no longer be based on free-market competition. That is, product and price would no longer be the main determinants of exchange transactions. Instead, the sale would go to the company that offered the largest payoff.

TRANSFER PRICING

A *transfer price* is the dollar basis used to quantify the transfer of goods or services from one segment of a business to another. Transfers can occur in domestic markets and/or international markets. When the transfer occurs across borders, a variety of legal and ethical issues arise for the entity. For example, the transfer price that is selected is subject to review by the taxing authorities in each jurisdiction. Typically, tax authorities attempt to ensure that the transfer price does not divert taxable income away from an entity in a particular country, especially one in a high-tax jurisdiction. Additionally, in a similar manner, the custom duties that are paid on imported products can be lowered. Regulators are concerned that the government is paid its fair share in taxes and duties. One measure of this is whether the transfer-price transactions are conducted at "arm's length"—that is, whether it represents a transaction between a willing buyer and a willing seller in a free market.

When business segments are designated as responsibility centers, the performance evaluation system should be adjusted to take into consideration any distortions in profitability or other measures of performance that result from transfer-price transactions. For example, if a segment in a high-corporate-tax jurisdiction sets an artificially low transfer price in a transaction with a related segment in a low-tax jurisdiction, the performance evaluation system should be adjusted to adequately reflect the true profitability of each segment. Otherwise, the transfer-price system can create counterproductive results and morale problems for the entity. Moreover, although the internal records may accurately portray the chosen transfer price, the external reports will not provide unbiased information, thereby bringing into question the reports' usefulness for external decision making.

International transfer pricing also affects relations with host countries. There are potential political, economic, and social effects of transfer-price transactions. These may impair the ability of a foreign entity to conduct operations in a particular country. On the other hand, the government of a host country may be reluctant to challenge the transfer-pricing practices of a foreign subsidiary because of concerns about the continued flow of international investment capital.

In 1990 a survey was conducted to determine the environmental variables that influence the transfer-pricing practices of Fortune 500 companies. The results clearly indicate that legal, political, and economic considerations far outweigh concerns about ethical issues. The top three factors are (1) overall profit to the company, (2) differentials in income tax rates and income tax legislation among countries, and (3) restrictions imposed by foreign countries on repatriation of profits or dividends. Only 2 of 20 variables have ethical implications. These are performance evaluation and the interests of local partners in foreign subsidiaries, and their rankings are 10 and 15, respectively.[3]

[3]Tang, Roger Y. W., "Transfer Pricing in the 1990s," *Management Accounting,* February 1992, pp. 22–26.

Quatish National
Petroleum Company

■

The developing nation of Quatish is located in North Africa. The country borders the Mediterranean, and it has valuable petroleum reserves under the sea. However, the Quatish National Petroleum Company has never engaged in offshore drilling. Its exploration and development work to date has been restricted to searching for petroleum deposits beneath the Sahara.

The government of Quatish asks the major oil companies around the world to bid on two separate projects. One is a $500 million joint-venture agreement with the Quatish National Petroleum Company to bring oil from beneath the Mediterranean to shore through pipelines for refining. The other is a $10 million contract to build a refinery to supplement the existing facilities of the Quatish National Petroleum Company. Bidding on the refinery contract will take place after selection of the joint-venture partner for oil development.

One of the companies bidding on the development contract is U.S. Oil & Gas, Inc. It is one of the largest producers and refiners of petroleum products in the United States. The president of U.S. Oil & Gas is Edward Kelly. Kelly has asked the company's external accountants to assist the company as consultants in the negotiations with the Quatishan government. The accountants have worked on these kinds of deals before, and they are very familiar with provisions of the Foreign Corrupt Practices Act that may be important in determining just what types of payments can be made to secure the contract.

Essentially, U.S. Oil & Gas proposes to enter into a 50:50 joint venture with a Quatishan national who would make all the local arrangements and find local workers to assist in the project. Joint-venture agreements are not unusual in this part of the world, since the local government wants to ensure that nationals are involved in any business venture that affects the natural resources of the country. One advantage of the joint-venture arrangement is that a local national, Ahmed Mibarry, can "run interference" for U.S. Oil & Gas and make the required facilitating payments.

Prior to submitting the bid on behalf of U.S. Oil & Gas, Tom Duffy, the consulting partner on the engagement, receives a telephone call from Mibarry. It seems that Mibarry has discovered through reliable sources that, in order to be awarded the oil exploration contract, U.S. Oil & Gas will have to make a $10 million payment to a government official. This official is the majority owner of the Quatish National Petroleum Company, and he has a great deal of influence on the decision-making process. Duffy informs Mibarry that he will have to call him back after he discusses the matter with Kelly and others in top management. Mibarry tells Duffy not to take too long, because there are at least two competitors waiting in the wings who are very willing to make the required payments.

Duffy meets with Kelly; George Greene, the chief financial officer; and Pete Johnson, the manager in charge of offshore oil production. Kelly tells Duffy that U.S. Oil & Gas does not do business that way. Kelly states, "Our company recognizes the need to 'grease the palms' of certain important government officials. However, we draw the line at bribing an official or any other person to secure business that, in our opinion, should be rightfully based on a fair bidding process." Greene adds that the payment suggested by Mibarry would violate the Foreign Corrupt Practices Act. Duffy knows this and supports the company in its decision. However, he repeats a comment that Mibarry made to him that may be worth considering. Mibarry asked Duffy, "Is it fair to expect us to follow U.S. ethical standards when you are coming to our country to do business with our people?"

Duffy, Kelly, and Greene discuss the matter at great length. They know that there are other bidders that represent countries where there are no restrictions on payments made in order to secure business. It is quite clear that U.S. Oil & Gas will lose out on the $500 million contract if it refuses to make the necessary payments, and it will likely be out of the running for the refinery contract, as well.

Kelly wonders whether there might be another way to handle the situation. He asks Duffy whether he has any ideas or suggestions. Duffy points out that he recalls a similar incident several years ago in a different country. In that situation, his client approached a government official who wanted a payoff and suggested instead that the company would employ a certain percentage of local nationals in return for the contract. The official accepted the alternative because he had ambitions to run for president of the country. The official believed that the announcement of his successful negotiation to have a large percentage of the work done by locals would ensure him of election victory. Duffy mentions that, because the proposal already stipulates the required percentage of local employees, it is not an option in this contract.

At this point Johnson comes up with an idea. He suggests that U.S. Oil & Gas offer to build the refinery for Quatish National Petroleum at no extra cost to the government. The decision to award both contracts to U.S. Oil & Gas should not be viewed as improper, because it is not unusual for one company to receive both contracts in a situation like this. The government just has to time its announcement so that it does not raise the suspicions of the other bidders. Johnson adds that, even if one of the competitors were to object, U.S. Oil & Gas could simply point out to them that it is not doing anything different than they would do. In fact, it would be providing a service to the government of Quatish.

Kelly really likes the idea. He states that Johnson's approach will not place the company in violation of the Foreign Corrupt Practices Act. However, Duffy is not so sure.

QUESTIONS

1. What is the relationship between compliance with the act and ethical behavior? Do you agree or disagree with the notion that the Foreign Corrupt Practices Act serves as a means to impose our ethical standards on other cultures?

2. Why do you think Tom Duffy is unsure about whether the company will be in violation of the Foreign Corrupt Practices Act if it offers to build the refinery at no additional cost to the Quatishan government? What recommendation should Duffy make to the client concerning Pete Johnson's idea?

WeSeal, Inc.

∎

WeSeal, Inc., is a U.S. multinational enterprise headquartered in Gary, Indiana. WeSeal recently expanded its overseas operations and now has foreign subsidiaries in 28 countries spread out over four geographic areas, including North America, South America, Europe, and Asia. WeSeal manufactures and sells automated equipment for applying sealants to containers and packaging materials. The company is decentralized, with each responsibility center having a great deal of autonomy over its decision making. However, centralized control is exercised when establishing transfer prices for the transfer of goods from one entity to another.

Recent technological advances in the manufacture of sealant equipment led the company to restrict the ability of foreign managers to buy equipment in the local markets. The current policy requires that each foreign subsidiary buy sealant equipment from WeSeal U.S.A. and then resell it to external customers in their local markets. This policy has created problems with some managers because the price they pay on transferred goods is no longer determined by market conditions or through negotiation. Instead, the company dictates the transfer price based on its objective of maximizing net income on a worldwide basis. Top management has sought to alleviate the concerns of individual managers by ensuring that appropriate adjustments will be made in the performance evaluation system. Another concern is the possibility that tension will develop between WeSeal subsidiaries and their host governments as a result of the transfer-pricing policy.

During the course of the audit of the December 31, 1995, financial statements, a memorandum was discovered by the auditors that casts doubt about the supportability of WeSeal's new transfer-pricing policy. It appears that the policy is being implemented by shifting income between countries in order to minimize the amount of taxes paid on worldwide profits. This memo is summarized on page 159.

Memo: Transfer-Pricing Policy

It is the company's intention to choose transfer prices that technically comply with Section 482 of the Internal Revenue Code. At the same time, every effort should be made to maximize net income on a worldwide basis. In order to meet the latter objective, the transfer-pricing policy should reflect corporate tax rate differentials in each geographic area.

Local managers should be informed of the new policy as soon as possible. Because it deviates from the prior transfer-pricing policy, which was based on market prices and negotiation with each subsidiary, we should be careful to assure each of the managers that the performance evaluation system will be adjusted accordingly. We should strongly discourage any attempt on their part to circumvent the policy by purchasing sealant equipment from external suppliers.

Roberta Lane is the partner in charge of the WeSeal audit for the professional services firm of Davis & Ellis LLP. Lane was informed of the memo by the audit manager on the job, Elliot Grayson. Lane is very concerned about the new transfer-pricing policy and possible implications of that policy for WeSeal. She knows that the IRS carefully scrutinizes this area of corporate income taxation. Lane decides to contact the tax department of the firm in order to learn more about the specifics of Section 482 of the Internal Revenue Code (IRC), which establishes tax rules for transfer pricing.

Lane meets with Lucy Evans, the firm's manager in charge of corporate tax research, to discuss the tax implications of WeSeal's new policy. Evans points out that Section 482 applies an arm's-length standard to transfer prices used in intracorporate transactions. The IRS recently amended this section of the tax regulations in order to increase its authority to allocate taxable income between entities under common control so that it would better reflect the income of the entities. Section 6662 also was amended to increase the documentation necessary to support a transfer price and avoid accuracy-related penalties. According to Evans, companies such as WeSeal that engage in a significant amount of transfer-price transactions are more likely to be subject to the extensive transfer-pricing analysis required under Sections 482 and 6662. Evans emphasizes the complicated nature of the tax requirements in this area. She suggests that the tax department prepare a memorandum outlining the new law and possible implications for clients, like WeSeal, that engage in the multinational transfer of tangible property from one entity to another. This memo appears in Appendix 1 on pages 160–162.

Lane puts down the memo and starts to consider the implications of WeSeal's transfer-pricing policy. She is aware of the riskiness of the new policy. However, the company does operate in some countries where the risk to the client is minimal because of lax enforcement of tax laws. In some of these countries, more concern exists about retaining foreign investment than complying with tax laws. In other countries, such as the United States, the United Kingdom, and Germany, there is a great deal of scrutiny of the tax laws. The risks are much greater in these countries. Lane wonders whether the company should be more selective in its transfer-pricing policy because of the political and legal risks.

QUESTIONS

1. If there were no guidance from the IRS, what are some of the ethical issues that should be considered in establishing a transfer-pricing policy? Do you think that WeSeal adequately considered these factors in developing its transfer-pricing policy as explained in the memo?

2. Carefully review the material in Appendix 1 and the final paragraph of the case. What stage of ethical reasoning do you think is illustrated by the memo prepared by the tax department? What stage is illustrated by the statements of Roberta Lane? Do you think that the firm has adequately considered the ethical issues in analyzing WeSeal's transfer-pricing policy?

APPENDIX 1
Memorandum on Changes to IRC Sections 482 and 6662 and Related Implications for Clients

The Internal Revenue Code (IRC) was recently amended in order to strengthen the ability of the IRS to reallocate income between related taxpayers when it is determined that the price used for the transfer of goods or services does not clearly reflect the income of any of the related taxpayers or when it is designed in order to evade taxes. A large adjustment under IRC Section 482 may trigger Section 6662 causing the taxpayer to have a "substantial valuation misstatement" or a "gross valuation misstatement." The accuracy-related penalties are 20% and 40%, respectively, for the underpayment of the tax as a result of the misstatement. The changes are described in greater detail in the following paragraphs.

Section 482

Regulations under IRC Section 482 continue to apply an arm's-length standard to transactions between taxpayers under common control. The IRS will not allocate income where the "best method" has been used to provide the most reliable measure of an arm's-length result in a particular situation. Implementation of the best-method rule requires that taxpayers use one of six methods for a controlled transfer of tangible property. These six methods are described below.*

1. **Comparable-Uncontrolled-Price Method:** The comparable uncontrolled price is a price determined by using comparable sales transactions between

---

*Crow, Stephen, and E. Sauls, "Setting the Right Transfer Price," *Management Accounting,* December 1994, pp. 41–47.

unrelated parties. Albeit a desirable method from the perspective of a market-based transaction, the comparable uncontrolled price is difficult to determine in situations where the selling entity does not have customers in the same geographic area as its foreign subsidiary.

2. **Resale-Price Method:** The resale price is the price to an unrelated party, less the related gross profit. The transfer price set under this method is the amount received by the foreign subsidiary on reselling the product to an uncontrolled outsider, reduced for an appropriate markup. This market-based method also is useful in pricing transferred goods. However, the problem described in item 1 also exists for this method. That is, the gross profit ratio used must be based on information on the profit ratios of unrelated companies distributing similar products. The documentation requirements of IRC Section 6662 are significant if this method is chosen.

3. **Cost-Plus Method:** This is the production costs plus gross profit on unrelated sales. This is a practical method for companies that manufacture a product. However, the documentation requirements also are significant because of the need to determine gross profit ratios of "comparable companies" that manufacture similar products.

4. **Comparable-Profits Method:** This method uses a price that yields gross profits comparable to those for other firms. The price can be determined by reference to industry averages. This method is practical when a product is not unique in the market. In such cases, reference to industry averages is both feasible and can be documented.

5. **Profits-Split Method:** This method relies on an allocation of the combined operating profits of the controlled entities on intercompany transfers. The determination of the profit to each entity is based on unit profits where uncontrolled entities are engaged in similar activities and have comparable products. The problem with this method is that product-line profit data often do not have enough detail to provide the required analysis and comparison.

6. **Other Methods:** Where none of the five specific methods above can "reasonably be applied" to a transfer, some other method that presents reasonable gross profits for the facts and circumstances can be used.

Section 6662

IRC Section 6662 provides for accuracy-related and fraud penalties in a number of situations, including substantial valuation misstatements resulting from transfer-price adjustments. This section establishes documentation requirements to support a transfer price. Under Section 6662 there are two accuracy-related penalties associated with underpayment of tax caused by incorrect transfer prices. These are described below.*

1. **Transactional Penalty.** A 20% penalty applies to valuation misstatements that result from transfer prices that are 200% or more (or 50% or less) than the correct price, as determined under Section 482. For example, if the correct transfer price is $100, a 20% penalty may apply if the entity chooses a transfer price of

---

*Lassar, Sharon S., and T. R. Skantz, "New Transfer Pricing Documentation Requirements and Penalties," *The CPA Journal,* April 1995, pp. 36–39.

$50 or less or $300 or more. The transactional penalty can be waived by the IRS if it determines that the U.S. entity exercised reasonable cause and good faith in setting transfer prices.

   2.   Net Adjustment Penalty.   The net adjustment penalty applies if transfer-price adjustments for the year that are required under Section 482 exceed certain thresholds. All transfer-price adjustments, including those subject to the transaction penalty, are netted in order to determine whether a net adjustment penalty applies. If the net adjustment exceeds the lesser of $5 million or 10% of gross receipts, a 20% penalty is imposed. If the net adjustment exceeds the lesser of $20 million or 20% of gross receipts, the penalty increases to 40%. For example, if the transfer-price adjustment results in a $20 million increase in U.S. taxable income then, assuming the IRS waived the transactional penalty, the net adjustment would be $9,072,000, or more than 45% of the increase in U.S. taxable income, determined as follows:

Section 482 adjustment ($20 million × 35% income tax rate)	$7,000,000
Gross valuation net adjustment penalty of 20% of the understatement ($7 million × 20%)	1,400,000
Estimated interest ($8.4 million × 8%)	672,000
Transactional penalty	$9,072,000

Other Considerations.   In addition to corporate income tax considerations, the following factors are relevant to transfer-price decisions.

   1.   Tariffs.   The increase or decrease in worldwide taxes because of a transfer-price implementation should be balanced against the effects of custom duties. In some cases, the higher duties that may occur as a result of a high transfer price to a purchasing subsidiary in a high-tax country more than offset the tax savings of the higher transfer price.

   2.   Political Considerations.   Because transfer prices have an effect on taxes and custom duties paid to local governments, the potential exists for transfer-price-related political problems in those countries that object to artificially high or low transfer prices.

   3.   International Financing.   Because the net income and cash flows of foreign subsidiaries may be affected by transfer prices, the ability of the entity to raise funds locally and in international markets can be similarly affected.

   4.   Performance Evaluation.   The management of foreign entities may object to artificially high transfer prices in cases where worldwide bonuses and other incentive payments are based on the operating profits of each entity.

Telecommunications, Inc.

■

Ed Keller is employed as an engineer for Telecommunications, Inc., a U.S. corporation. A recent graduate with a master's degree in engineering, he has only been with the company for six months. He chose to work for Telecommunications because of the opportunity to travel throughout the world and because he was impressed by the company's reputation for quality service and high moral standards.

Telecommunications, Inc., is a global leader in the information technology field. Recently, the government of a Latin American country awarded the company a multimillion-dollar contract for the development of a new fiber-optic system that would speed the transmission of information throughout the world. The fiber-optic system was already in place in several other countries, including the United States. Telecommunications was selected as the prime contractor, following a competitive bidding process with two other multinational enterprises.

As the prime contractor, Telecommunications was expected to select subcontractors to perform work that the company itself did not feel qualified to perform. According to Telecommunications's contract with the foreign government, only Latin American companies could be selected for subcontract work. One such subcontract for electrical and mechanical work was awarded to Techno Corporation. It was not as well established as some of the other bidding companies. However, Techno was the only company that could do the work in a manner that would satisfy the engineering specifications that had been established for the job.

During lunch at the office one day, Keller was talking to several of the more senior members of the engineering staff of Telecommunications, who told him about their recent trip to Latin America. They visited four countries in two weeks, and all their expenses were paid for by Techno. Keller knew that Techno had just been awarded the contract for electrical and mechanical work on the fiber-optic system. He questioned the engineering staff members about the propriety of accepting an all-expense paid trip from a major contractor of the company. He was told that it was common practice for Latin American companies to make gestures of gratitude, such as free travel and entertainment. One of the senior engineers, Mike Stone, stated: "There's nothing wrong with accepting such an offer. After all, the offer of free travel was made after the decision to accept the bid of Techno. We were not responsible for making that decision. All we did was to establish the engineering specifications for the job."

Keller was very curious about the Techno contract and the entire bidding process, so he approached Sam Jennings, the head of the internal audit department of Telecommunications. Jennings was a good friend of Keller's family and was the first person to contact Keller in graduate school about interviewing with Telecommunications. He asked Jennings to explain the way in which the decision was made to accept the Techno bid. Keller suggested that exposure to the decision-making process could be quite useful to him as a new employee. Some day he would be directly involved in developing engineering specifications for a job. Keller told Jennings that this could be a great learning experience for him.

Jennings agreed to explain the process to Keller. Before doing so, however, he told Keller that he is always concerned about the bidding process whenever it involves a foreign contract. That is because of the provisions of the Foreign Corrupt Practices Act (FCPA) that prohibit payments designed to influence the decisions of foreign officials. Although there was no evidence that any such payments were made in the current situation, it was a sensitive issue for Telecommunications because of previous disclosures of illegal payments made by other companies in the industry. (Background information about the FCPA and a summary of its provisions related to unlawful influence are presented in "Ethics in the International Environment."

Keller learned during Jennings's explanation of the process that Techno's bid was actually the highest one submitted. However, Techno was the only bidding company that could supply the material needed for the job. If Telecommunications had accepted one of the lower bids, it would have meant that the company would have had to sacrifice product quality for cost savings. While the cost savings were significant, both Richard Kimble, the engineering division manager, and Bob Gerard, the vice president for engineering, were in agreement that only Techno could do the job in a manner that would be consistent with the stated engineering specifications. Engineering considerations overrode cost factors in the decision-making process.

Keller then brought up for discussion with Jennings what he believed was an apparent conflict of interest resulting from some engineers' accepting all-expense-paid trips from Techno. Jennings informed Keller that he had already investigated that relationship and did not find any violation of Telecommunications's code of ethics. The code did prohibit relationships that could influence actions or give the appearance of being capable of influencing actions. However, no evidence existed that the engineering specifications were purposely written in such a way to preclude subcontractors other than Techno. Additionally, the decision to accept

Techno's bid was made jointly by Kimble and Gerard, neither of whom received any free trips or other gifts from Techno.

Keller felt better about the situation after discussing it with Jennings. Still, he wondered about the values of the engineers who accepted offers of free travel from the client entity.

QUESTIONS

1. What behavioral and ethical issues are raised by the facts of this case with respect to the potential effect on the operations of Telecommunications, Inc.?
2. Do you think Ed Keller is right to be concerned about the values of the engineers who accepted offers of free travel?

END-OF-TEXT ASSIGNMENTS

End-of-Text Assignments

■

I. Research Assignment

Several cases in the book raise questions about the materiality of a transaction or an event. For example, in the Linex Corporation case a judgment is made by the external auditors about the materiality of a litigation uncertainty and the need for financial statement disclosure of the event. In the Supreme Designs case the issue is one of cumulative effect in judging the materiality of improper cash disbursements.

A. Briefly summarize the guidance available in the accounting literature regarding materiality determinations. Is there one standard by which to judge materiality or are there many such standards?

B. What should be the role of the ethical norms that were discussed in the second section of the book in evaluating the need to report a possible material business transaction or event? Should ethical behavior vary, depending on the materiality of the issue involved?

C. In the Cubbies Cable case there was a difference of opinion between the external auditors and the client about whether to record in the current period the $2 million profit on the sale-leaseback transaction or to defer this amount and amortize it over the leaseback period. The facts of the case imply that the client's position is motivated by a desire to make the financial statements look better than they really are, in anticipation of future borrowing. Assume that the $2 million amount is determined not to be material and that, therefore, the auditors decide to go along with the clients' position. Evaluate the ethics of the auditors' decision to support the client's position.

II. Case Situation

You work for an accounting firm that has a policy of ignoring differences of opinion with a client on accounting issues whenever the amount of the transaction or event is below a threshold level. In other words, for certain clients the firm has determined that a difference of opinion that involves an amount of $100,000 or less is not material. Assume that this is a legitimate position for the firm to take.

A difference of opinion develops with a client regarding the proper amount to record as the market decline in the value of inventory. The auditors believe it should be $150,000. However, the client's reaction is that there is no way it can go along with such a large write-down. The client agrees only to a $50,000 write-down. After a great deal of discussion among the auditors (during which a variety of opinions are expressed), the partner in charge of the engagement decides that $100,000 can be ignored under the firm's policy. Therefore, the firm goes along with the client's position and only records a $50,000 write-down of inventory.

A. Evaluate the ethical propriety of the engagement partner's position in light of the firm's policy.

B. Divide the class into two groups and have each group present verbal arguments to support the following positions:

  1. Go along with the client's position and only record a $50,000 write-down, because it is consistent with firm policy to do so.

  2. Refuse to go along with the client and insist on recording the full $150,000 write-down, because the client's position is one that cannot be justified from an ethical reasoning perspective.

III. Role-Playing Exercises

Choose students to role-play any one of the following situations that occur in selected cases in the book:

A. Ed Giles and Susan Regas

Role-play the meeting between Herb Morris and Ed Giles at which they discussed the client's concerns about the high level of billings that may have resulted from Giles's relationship with Regas. Bring Regas into the meeting after a period of time.

B. Edvid, Inc.

Role-play the meeting between Charles Hutton and the practice director of the firm to discuss the client's ultimatum that either the firm support Edvid's position on revenue recognition or the company will seek proposals from other accounting firms. Bring the CFO of Edvid into the meeting after a period of time.

C. Cubbies Cable

Role-play the meeting between Ernie Binks, John Kessinger, and Ron Hundley, where Binks stands by his position that all of the profit on the sale should be deferred and amortized over the leaseback period.

D. Creative Toys, Inc.

Role-play a meeting between Sharon Browne, Edie Wasler, and Sid Gurchick, at which Browne is to give her final position on the inventory write-down.

E. Quatish National Petroleum Company

Role-play a final discussion between Tom Duffy, Ed Kelly, George Greene, and Pete Johnson, during which a final decision will be made regarding whether to go forward with Johnson's idea of offering to build the refinery at no extra cost to the government in return for the $500 million contract.